REACH FOR THE INFINITE

Edmund Banyard

Ah, but a man's reach should exceed his grasp,
or what's a heaven for?

Robert Browning
Andrea Del Sarto

Other books by Edmund Banyard published by NCEC:
The Flame
A Fistful of Fivers
A Packet of Crackers
The Maker of Things (with Graham Bishop-Hunt)
Turn but a Stone
Heaven and Charing Cross

Cover design and text illustrations: Phillip Vernon
Cover photograph: Elizabeth Bruce

Published by:
National Christian Education Council
1020 Bristol Road
Selly Oak
Birmingham
B29 6LB

British Library Cataloguing in Publication Data:
A catalogue record for this book is available from the British Library.

ISBN 0-7197-0969-5

First published 2000

© Edmund Banyard 2000

Edmund Banyard has asserted his right under the Copyright, Designs and Patents Act, 1988, to be identified as Author of this Work.

Typeset by Phillip Vernon
Printed and bound by Biddles, Guildford, UK

Contents

Contents

Preface

However much I strive through prayers, meditations, songs or dialogues to express the nearness, the relevance, the surprises and, above all, the all-embracing love of the Eternal God, I am still seeking after wonders that are far beyond me. Thus, *Reaching for the Infinite*.

The framework I have used here is *The Revised Common Lectionary*, in the hope that the book will prove a useful tool for all who use this lectionary week by week; but I trust that it will also be a book for those who like to dip into a volume without asking whether the piece is related to the biblical passages recommended for that particular moment in time.

I have long found lectionaries a useful stimulant, though sometimes they have caused me to ask, 'Why on earth did they select this passage and omit that one?' and I haven't always discovered a satisfactory answer! However I can testify that lectionaries have widened my perspective, given some shape to my devotional life and occasionally opened up paths which I might not otherwise have taken.

Two previous volumes, *Turn but a Stone* and *Heaven and Charing Cross*, followed a lectionary which has now been superseded. The material here is fresh, which, I hope you can agree, only emphasizes the vastness of the riches which can be dug out of the fertile ground of the Holy Scriptures.

The gospel does not change, but the framework in which we have to interpret the gospel is changing all the time and so this book is offered as a contribution which may be used both for personal devotion and in corporate acts of worship. If it encourages you to go on and write something for yourself, so much the better.

Edmund Banyard
Diss, Norfolk
January 2000

Acknowledgements and Abbreviations

Some pieces have been published previously, particularly in *All Year Round* (Churches Together in Britain and Ireland). Where they are extracted from a larger work the source is indicated below and they are reprinted with the permission of the original publishers.

Stainer and Bell Ltd,
23 Gruneison Road,
Finchley, London N3 1DZ
So you challenge the popular line, page 31
The Battle
Another man's load, page 65
One Friday In Eternity
The Centurion at the cross, page 66
Conversation in the Upper Room, page 71
Out Of This World
Shout it in the street, page 81
The Super Skyscraper
Mine is a very little world, page 88
Whatever next?, page 107
I've said it before, page 114
If you cried out in rage, page 177
One Friday

The following are available only in
Manuscript
Lord, reshape the lives we offer, page 38
Go not in search of miracles, page 130
Lord of the storm clouds, page 161
Cuthbert
Be strong in the Lord, page 137
Ragman

NCEC
At the birth of all that has ever
been created, page 97
The Maker Of Things

Radius
Christ Church & Upton Chapel,
Kennington Road,
London SE1 7QP
Let a star shine out through the
darkness, page 14
George
O Lord, forgive, page 47
There's a man on a cross, page 70
It seemed they had come to the
end of the way, page 73
Mary was the first, page 80
Turn off the news, page135
Upside Down And Inside Out

We are grateful for permission
to quote from the following
Bible versions:

AV	Authorized Version
GNB	Good News Bible
NJB	New Jerusalem Bible
REB	Revised English Bible

Extracts from the Authorized Version of the Bible (The King James Bible), the rights in which are vested in the Crown, are reproduced by permission of the Crown's Patentee, Cambridge University Press.

Good News Bible, second edition©American Bible Society 1992. The Bible Societies /Harper Collins.

The New Jerusalem Bible, published and copyright 1985 by Darton, Longman and Todd Ltd and les Editions du Cerf, used by permission of the publishers.

Extracts from The Book of Common Prayer, the rights in which are vested in the Crown, are reproduced by permission of the Crown's Patentee, Cambridge University Press.

Revised English Bible ©Oxford University Press and Cambridge University Press 1989.

The compiler and publishers express thanks for permission to use copyright items. Every effort has been made to trace copyright owners but if any rights have been inadvertently overlooked, the necessary corrections will gladly be made in subsequent editions.

Wake us, Lord, wake us

Pray for the peace of Jerusalem. (Psalm 122.6 REB)
It is high time for you to wake out of sleep. (Romans 13.11 REB)

Jerusalem is a battleground
peopled by fragmented communities.
Jew quarrels with Jew,
Arab with Arab,
and Jew and Arab bitterly contend
for possession of the sacred city.
There is hostility among Christians
over 'rights' within the Holy Places,
and the pattern is repeated
with endless variations
wherever there is human habitation.
Shall Jerusalem ever know peace?
Shall the world ever know peace?
How long, O Lord, how long?

Wake us, Lord, wake us
make us face up to
the fear,
the pride,
and the small-mindedness
which fuel our reluctance
even to try to understand
other cultures,
other hopes, other ambitions.
We admit that we have been slow to respond
to the voice which calls us
to pray for, to work for,
and to make personal sacrifices for
- the peace of Jerusalem,
- the peace of our own people,
- the peace of the world.
Wake us, Lord, wake us,
and stir us into prayerful action
that we may not be ashamed at your coming.

Couldn't you give us just a little warning?

First Sunday in Advent. Year B

> Be on your guard, keep watch. You do not know when the moment is coming. (Mark 13.33 REB)
> Why did you not tear asunder the heavens and come down, that, when you appeared, the mountains might shake? (Isaiah 64.1 REB)

You'll always be welcome, Lord,
of course you will;
but this not knowing
quite how or when to expect you
does create just a little bit of a problem.

Say you turn up unexpectedly one evening;
well, we don't always hear the door
when the television's on,
and it generally is.

And as to seeing you out in the street;
what with folks with clip boards conducting surveys,
holding collecting boxes
or plain begging,
we try to avoid strangers.

There's the telephone of course,
but so many calls are trying to sell
home improvements or insurance
that if we don't quickly recognize the voice
we tend to put the receiver down.

You'll always be welcome, Lord,
of course you will,
but it would so help
if you could give us a little warning of your coming.

From looking without seeing,
from hearing without understanding,
and from being unwilling to break out of cosy routines;
Good Lord, deliver us.

With power and great glory

> Then they will see the Son of Man coming in a cloud with power and great glory. (Luke 21.27 REB)

Almighty God,
in the wilderness years
your people only perceived your glory in a cloud,
half hidden, half revealed.

At the coming of your Christ
it was not to a packed audience
of crowned heads and ministers of state
that the angels sang,
but to a group of shepherds.

Thirty years later
it was not on a war horse
that Jesus entered Jerusalem
but on a donkey
and he came to his kingdom
not on a throne, but on a cross.

As we contemplate
the second coming of our Lord,
'with power and great glory'
are we making a mistake
in looking for a cataclysmic event?
Are we confusing the way you reveal
your power and glory
with the very different trappings
of earthly pomp and state?

**God of so many surprises,
we thank you that you have a way
of turning normal expectations on their head
so that your power and glory may be revealed
as you quietly break through all obstacles
to enter into and transform an erring human life.
Come, Lord Jesus, come;
enter into and possess our lives
and make your power and glory known in us.**

3

Our God is a biased God

Second Sunday in Advent. Year A

With justice he will judge the poor and defend the humble. (Isaiah 11.4 REB)
Prove your repentance by the fruit you bear. (Matthew 3.8 REB)

The voice which cries
in our own particular wilderness
calls for a change in the way
we see and value things
in our high production,
high consumption society;
in our success driven world.

Our God is a biased God,
biased in favour of the poor and needy;
biased in favour of the misfits,
the rejects,
the rebels;
biased in favour of the people
who've made a thorough mess of their lives.
And the voice cries:
'Will you not see them as I see them?'
'Will you not care for them as I care?'

Lord,
if you discount parking and speeding offences
we're a pretty law-abiding group of people,
but,
at times,
you do give us the uncomfortable feeling
that being law-abiding isn't quite enough.
Help us to understand better
what you mean by righteousness and justice.
Help us to make your values our values,
and strengthen our will
to witness and work for your ways
by the things we count important
and the manner in which
we live our everyday lives.

Beyond time, yet in all time

Second Sunday in Advent. Year B

> Clear a road through the wilderness for the Lord. (Isaiah 40.3 REB)
> In the Lord's sight one day is like a thousand years and a thousand years like one day. (2 Peter 3.8 REB)

Caught in the web of time,
how can we comprehend
you, who are beyond time,
you to whom past, present and future
are all one eternal 'Now'?

Yet you allow yourself
to be ensnared in time's web.
You were present in a winter birth in Bethlehem.
You 'suffered under Pontius Pilate'.

You are the God who is closer than we know.
Though you seek meeting
and bid us prepare for your coming
you are already amongst us,
always have been,
always will be.

God beyond time,
yet meeting us in time;
even as we seek to clear a way for you
through the wilderness of our living
you are already at our side.
You are the God who broke into history,
you are the God of the present moment
and you are the God who is yet to come.
You were in our yesterdays,
you are in our 'now',
and you will be in our tomorrows.
God ever present,
God of all generations,
thanks be to you
for your unfailing love.

A strong deliverer

Second Sunday in Advent. Year C

> He has raised for us a strong deliverer ... out of the hands of all that hate us ... and to guide our feet into the way of peace. (Luke 1.69,71,79 REB)

Saviour Lord,
help us to free ourselves
from the fallacy
that to save us
you must destroy others.
Teach what it means
that you come as Saviour of the world,
not just our small part of it;
that you reach out to all men and women,
not just those who think and do as we do.

Help us to grasp the hard lesson
that your saving love
can embrace men and women
in whom we see no redeeming features,
men and women whom we would write off
as utterly worthless.

If there is hatred or bitterness
in our own hearts, Lord;
if there are those of whom we say,
'We cannot forgive';
deal gently with us,
grant us a little more of your Spirit
that we may feel something of the love
you have for them;
and that our feet may truly
be led in the way of your peace.

Not quite what was expected

> Your God comes to save you. (Isaiah 35.4 REB)
> Are you the one who is to come? (Matthew 11.3 REB)

Even John the Baptist,
who fearlessly proclaimed
the way of the Lord
in the Jordan valley
and was thrown into prison
and executed
for attacking evil in high places;
even John the Baptist
found that he had his doubts,
asking: 'Are you really the one who is to come?'

John was eagerly looking for God to break into life,
but when it happened he was troubled.
It was something so very, very different
from what he had been expecting.

**Lord Jesus Christ,
grant us the humility and the insight
to be able to recognize
when you are speaking to us,
though it be through words or actions
which challenge our assumption
that we already know what we should be doing.
Make us more aware of your presence
in everyday experiences;
and enable us
to recognize your call
when it comes,
whether through newspaper article,
Bible passage,
a stirring call to action
or quiet inner promptings.
Open our eyes to the signs
which declare that your kingdom
is already in our midst
and make us more ready to be led into new ways.**

An authentic voice?

Third Sunday in Advent. Year B

He has sent me to announce good news to the humble. (Isaiah 61.1 REB)
I am a voice crying in the wilderness. (John 1.23 REB)

Was John the only preacher in the Jordan valley
or did he have to compete with other voices?
There were, of course,
>   no radio channels broadcasting round the clock;
>   no newspapers;
>   no mobile phones,
>   fax machines,
>   e-mail or internet;
but these were unsettled times,
with many revolutionary spirits abroad.
How did those who flocked to John
recognize that in this man
there was an authentic
Word from God?

There are so many many voices
urging me
to do this,
to do that,
to grasp this opportunity,
enjoy that new experience.
Help me, Lord, I pray,
to distinguish which voices
should be heeded
and which ignored.
Give me the wisdom
to recognize among them
your voice,
your Word,
however startling the message,
whatever the manner of its delivery.

The power that saves

Fear not, Zion... The Lord your God is in your midst. (Zephaniah 3.16-17 REB)
With joy you will all draw water from the wells of deliverance. (Isaiah 12.3 REB)
The Lord is near; do not be anxious, but in everything make your requests known
to God in prayer and petition with thanksgiving. (Philippians 4.5-6 REB)
Vipers' brood! Who warned you to escape from the wrath that is to come?
(Luke 3.7 REB)

Much as I know
that I need to heed John's message,
calling for a change of heart,
a change of direction;
something in me resists.
I am suspicious of those clear-cut distinctions
between good and evil, right and wrong.
They take no account of the grey areas
where for so much of the time
I have to pick my way.

It is the other message which overwhelms me:
the word of a God who accepts me as I am,
who loves me as I am,
who comes as rescuer, as Saviour.
This it is which gives me the will to change.
This it is which gives me the power to change.

Almighty and eternal God,
we have no claim on you,
but you have every claim on us,
for you have fashioned us
and given us the capacity to become
truly free persons.
You have reached out to save us
from the insidious grip of evil
and you have honoured us
by calling us to your service.
Lord, what can we say,
what response can we possibly make
to these all-embracing
initiatives of your love?
What can we say except,
'Lord, we are yours,
may we remain yours for ever'?

9

A sign of hope?

Fourth Sunday in Advent. Year A

> Not content with wearing out the patience of men, must you also wear out the patience of my God? Because you do, the Lord of his own accord will give you a sign. (Isaiah 7.13-14 REB)
>
> A virgin will conceive and bear a son, and he shall be called 'Emmanuel', a name which means 'God is with us'. (Matthew 1.23 REB)

Ahaz had already decided
what he would do;
the last thing he wanted
was a sign from heaven.
Nevertheless a sign was given.
It should have been a sign of hope:
instead, it served to emphasize
the folly of the way which he had chosen.

**Beyond the crowded shops,
the incessant piped carols,
the Christmas TV spectaculars,
the eating, drinking and partying;
beyond all the strident noise:
give us the understanding, Lord,
to recognize the meaning
of the child born in a stable.
Teach us again that your salvation
reaches us through simple things:
- the love of a mother,
- the needs of a child,
- a life lived for others;
and help us in our own time
to recognize, to trust
and to respond
to your signs of hope.**

A travelling God

> ...since I brought Israel up from Egypt; I lived in a tent. (2 Samuel 7.6 REB)
> My soul tells out the greatness of the Lord. (Luke 1.46 REB)
> To the only wise God through Jesus Christ be glory for endless ages! Amen.
> (Romans 16.27 REB)

It was the tent of meeting
that symbolized your presence
during the wilderness years;
a mobile dwelling
for a travelling God,
a God never left behind by changing times.

We build and maintain our churches,
carefully plan our worship
and order our church life;
but have you moved on?
Are we getting left behind?

Because we are slow to move
are you calling others,
unknown to us,
to proclaim the greatness of the Lord?
Are you sending out apostles
whom we have failed to recognize
to declare your glory?

Travelling God,
always journeying with your people;
always ready to spring new surprises;
as we celebrate the coming of our Saviour
help us to recognize
the mighty works you are doing in our own time
and give us the grace to be willing
to be part of them;
to be ready
when you call us,
to say with Mary,
'I am the Lord's servant,
do with me as you will.'

Blessing is not to be taken lightly

Fourth Sunday in Advent. Year C

> Of all women you are the most blessed. (Luke 1.42 NJB)

The time of worship draws to a close
and we prepare to return to the world
with a final blessing,
a 'wrap around' source of comfort,
a defence against unknown ills —
> *'The blessing of God Almighty,*
> *Father, Son and Holy Spirit*
> *Go with you and remain with you...'*
We go out strengthened, reassured:
God is with us.

And yet it can be a fearful thing
to be singled out for blessing.
To be blessed above all women meant for Mary
> a child conceived before marriage;
> giving birth to that child in an outhouse,
> watching that same child grow
> to strike out on a course of life
> which could threaten the whole family
> and then to see him crucified.

But not only Mary.
Saints and martyrs are regarded as greatly blessed,
but they hardly have peaceful lives.

Lord, we need your blessing
to make us whole, fulfilled people;
but if that blessing should lead us
into strange and difficult paths
we ask that you will strengthen
our faith and our trust
that we may accept what you would do with us,
so that, blessed,
we may in turn be blessing to others.

God with us

Nativity of the Lord (Christmas Day). Years A, B & C

> So the Word became flesh; he made his home among us. (John 1.14 REB)

Helpless,
vulnerable,
exposed;
a frail human baby born in a cattle shed —
in such a manner
God made his home among us,
that we might be drawn to him
through his very defencelessness.

There was no one to deny entry
to that Bethlehem stable;
no security locks,
no guards,
no barriers of any kind;
indeed, in Christ,
God came to break all barriers down.

To respond to that love
which risks all in reaching out to us
we surely must also take risks
in reaching out to others.
Risk being misunderstood;
risk having our overtures rejected;
risk becoming vulnerable, defenceless.

How else
can the true Christmas message
be transmitted?
How else
can the word of peace,
the word of reconciliation,
become flesh in us?

God with us

Let a star shine out through the darkness,
let a new song greet the dawn,
let the whole earth hear good tidings,
for a Saviour has been born.
Sing, sing, sing to the Lord,
let the earth be filled with his glory.

Let the wise set out on their journey,
let the watchers hail his birth,
let the heavens ring with rejoicing,
for a Saviour's come to earth.
Sing, sing, sing to the Lord,
let the earth be filled with his glory.

Let the air be vibrant with music,
spread the news without delay,
let the joy be universal,
for a Saviour's born today.
Sing, sing, sing to the Lord,
let the earth be filled with his glory.
(From *George*)

**Thanks be to God
who has come to meet us in a human life,
bringing light to our darkness,
hope to our despair,
joy to ease our sorrows
and peace which springs from the knowledge
that, despite all our follies,
we are held fast
in an unfailing love
through Jesus Christ our Lord.
Thanks be to God.**

Was there no other way?

> I shall recount the Lord's unfailing love. (Isaiah 63.7 REB)
> Because he himself has passed through the test of suffering, he is able to help those who are in the midst of their test. (Hebrews 2.18 REB)
> When Herod realized that the astrologers had tricked him he flew into a rage, and gave orders for the massacre of all the boys aged two years or under, in Bethlehem and throughout the whole district. (Matthew 2.16 REB)

The Christ Child
is saved from Herod's wrath,
God's purposes have not been thwarted;
but — at what a price!
Our hearts go out to the families
whose children were slaughtered.
They had no warning,
no means of escape.
Did this really have to be?
Was there no other way?

Even as we praise you, Lord,
we cannot escape the darker side of life.
Is it right that we should be rejoicing
in blessings received
while others are engulfed in tragedy?
We find it hard to understand
the suffering so many have to endure.
We hold to the fact that in Jesus
you identified yourself with the weak,
the helpless,
and with all who endure pain or sorrow.
We still cannot understand
why the world is the way it is,
but we do believe that you are calling us
to play our part in carrying on the work of Jesus.
Stiffen our resolve, we pray,
to give help in his name
wherever we have opportunity to do so.

Through darkness the light still shines

First Sunday after Christmas. Year B

> I have seen with my own eyes the deliverance you have made ready.
> (Luke 2.30-31 REB)
> This child is destined to be a sign that will be rejected; and you too will be
> pierced to the heart. (Luke 2.34-35 REB)

Lord, now lettest thou thy servant depart in peace,
according to thy word.
For mine eyes have seen thy salvation,
which thou hast prepared
before the face of all people.
To be a light to lighten the Gentiles
and to be the glory of thy people Israel. (Book of Common Prayer)

So through the generations,
in the familiar words of the Nunc Dimittis,
men and women have echoed Simeon's song
of thankfulness and praise.
In his arms he held the child
destined to be the Saviour of the world,
yet it was a bittersweet vision
which had been granted to Simeon.
He saw that joy would be mixed with sorrow,
that this child would grow to face rejection and suffering
before, through his sacrifice,
our deliverance could be effected.

Lord, we thank you
that though Christmas is over
the Christmas message of a Saviour remains.
We thank you
that though all the presents
have been opened
the greatest gift of all
can still bring us joyous surprises.
We may for a time have eaten well,
if not always wisely;
but through your sacrificial giving of yourself
you offer us the bread and water of life
that we may be sustained all our days
and by your mercy be brought at the last
to your eternal kingdom.

The child in the Temple

> Listening to them and putting questions. (Luke 2.46 REB)
> Did you not know that I was bound to be in my Father's house? (Luke 2.49 REB)

A.   Did you notice the boy who suddenly appeared at the teaching sessions in the Temple?

B.   Could hardly miss him with the searching questions he asked. He's certainly been taught by a good Rabbi.

A.   I fear for that boy.

B.   His parents collected him this afternoon. Father's a carpenter from Nazareth. They didn't realize he wasn't with their party returning after the festival. He's on his way home now. No need to worry.

A.   It wasn't that; no, I fear for his future.

B.   How so? A bright boy like that should do well for himself.

A.   The boy's in love with God and thinks of the Temple as God's house. What will happen when he realizes the truth?

B.   The truth?

A.   The politics, the scheming, the infighting among the priests; the awful emptiness behind the carefully orchestrated rituals.

B.   You're laying it on a bit thick, aren't you? People grow to accept that that's how things are.

A.   He won't. He's too intelligent and too sincere. When he comes to recognize the hypocrisy behind it all he'll either become a militant atheist or...

B.   Or what?

A   I don't know, but I'm sure he won't let things rest. That's why I fear for him.

Heavenly Father,
we hold before you all young people
growing up with hopes, ideals
and dreams of doing good.
Defend them, we pray,
from cynicism, from despair
and from all that would destroy
their sense of purpose;
and so deal with them
that they may grow to know, to love
and to serve you all their days.

A pipe dream?

Second Sunday after Christmas. Years A, B & C

> So the Word became flesh; he made his home among us, and we saw his glory, such glory as befits the Father's only Son, full of grace and truth. (John 1.14 REB) He has made known to us his secret purpose ... namely, that the universe, everything in heaven and on earth, might be brought into a unity in Christ. (Ephesians 1.9-10 REB)

'And God said...'
So simple — so breathtaking!
The Word is spoken
and the process begun
by which the universe is brought into being.

'So the Word became flesh...'
A second wonder.
Again the Word:
expressed, and meeting us now
in a human life.

Add a third marvel!
It is the will and purpose of God,
who spoke the creating Word
that the whole universe,
together with whatever lies beyond the universe,
might ultimately be brought into a unity in Christ...

To us earthbound creatures, Lord,
even a totally harmonious church
seems a pipe dream;
how much more difficult
to conceive of the whole of creation
in perfect harmony.
Yet you tell us that this is the goal,
and that making it happen
is the work of Christ,
and so our work.
Do not allow us to lose sight of this vision;
do not allow us to cease from believing
that, with you,
these things really are possible.

Rise and shine!

Arise, shine, Jerusalem, for your light has come; and over you the glory of the Lord has dawned. (Isaiah 60.1 REB)
Through the gospel the Gentiles are joint heirs with the Jews, part of the same body, sharers together in the promise made in Christ Jesus. (Ephesians 3.6 REB)
Then they returned to their own country by another route, for they had been warned in a dream not to go back to Herod. (Matthew 2.12 REB)

'Arise, shine!'
but they had no desire to rise and shine,
the people of Isaiah's Jerusalem;
they were more than willing
that God's light should shine on them,
but they had no intention of reflecting that light
for the benefit of others.

Centuries passed.
Strangers from other cultures
came to Jerusalem,
Herod's Jerusalem,
seeking a new-born, God-given Saviour.
The king had no time for divine initiatives;
to him they were threats rather than promises.
So after the strangers had found the child
and worshipped him,
instead of returning to Herod,
they slipped quietly away
and returned home by a little-used route,
carefully avoiding the border guards.

God of all peoples,
forgive us when we try to set arbitrary limits
on the reach of your salvation.
Forgive us when we assert
that our way is the only acceptable way
to enter your kingdom.
Broaden our vision,
and help us so to grow in the warmth of your love
that we may come to be reflectors
of the light of life
to any whose lives are still in darkness.

Jesus joined the queue

Baptism of the Lord. Year A

> I have formed you, and destined you to be a light for peoples, a lamp for nations, to open eyes that are blind. (Isaiah 42.6-7 REB)
> This is my beloved Son, in whom I take delight. (Matthew 3.17 REB)

Jesus joined the queue:
just one among many
of those seeking baptism from John.
It was as he came up out of the water
that he heard the Father's voice,
'This is my beloved Son,
in whom I take delight',
but even then he knew
that the path which lay ahead
would be a stony one.

The Chosen People
had failed to respond to their calling
to be a light for all peoples;
Jesus,
seeking no privileges,
choosing to be one among many,
ready to lose himself in the service of others,
willingly accepted the whole burden
of being the Servant of the Lord,
and a light for the world.

Lord Jesus Christ, your humility shames us.
We can so easily get upset
when we feel that people fail to value
what we have to offer,
or when others are praised and encouraged
and we are ignored.
Forgive us
when we think too much about ourselves,
and point us again to our calling
as your people
to be servants, willingly, for your sake.

Light for the world

> God said, 'Let there be light,' and there was light; and God saw the light was good. (Genesis 1.3-4 REB)
> And a voice came from heaven: 'You are my beloved Son; in you I take delight.' (Mark 1.11 REB)

First came light,
and with light came
the opportunity
to perceive shapes and colours,
assess distances,
recognize dangers
and marvel at wonders;
the opportunity
to distinguish the desirable
from the undesirable;
the ability to see and to choose.

Yet, having sight,
men and women still fail to see;
and, having light,
still move in darkness.
So came Jesus,
and the Word which called light into being
shone through a human life;
light for the world,
light for the dark inner recesses of the soul.

**Light-giving God,
when our world is dark,
especially if the darkness is of our own making,
break through whatever clouds engulf us,
that we may walk once again
in the light which you give.
And if we do stray from the path of life,
so deal with us in your mercy
that we may be brought
safely back into the way once again.**

A baptism of fire?

Baptism of the Lord. Year C

This is the word of the Lord, the word of your Creator ... Have no fear, for I have redeemed you; I call you by name; you are mine ... when you pass through rivers they will not overwhelm you; walk through fire, and you will not be scorched. (Isaiah 43.1-2 REB)
I baptize you with water; but there is one coming who is mightier than I am ...
He will baptize you with the Holy Spirit and with fire. (Luke 3.16 REB)

With fire?
What sort of baptism is this?
Baptism with water we understand:
an infant brought for Christian baptism
by loving parents,
or believers going under the water
and professing their faith
in the presence of a supportive Christian congregation.
But fire!
True, fire gives warmth and light
but it also consumes and destroys;
is being 'baptized into Christ'
likely to be such a searing experience?

**In your earthly ministry, Lord,
you had no easy passage;
you passed through the fires
of bitter hostility, torture
and cruel death,
and many of your servants
have trodden a similar path.
We pray for those who are today
enduring such a baptism.
May they know your love
so enfolding them
that, though passing through fire,
they may not be consumed.**

Sharing the good news

> Patiently I waited for the Lord; ... he set my feet on rock and gave me a firm footing. (Psalm 40.1-2 REB)
> 'There is the Lamb of God!' ... 'We have found the Messiah.' (John 1.36,41 REB)

John the Baptist
pointed Andrew to Jesus
and Andrew
passed on the news
to his brother Peter.
So the process began
by which the company
of the followers of Jesus grew,
as one shared with another
the good news
that God was meeting them
in their everyday lives,
just where they were.

**Heavenly Father,
we believe we can trust you
in the confidence
that, however difficult the way ahead may be,
you will be in it with us.
But we also believe
that your help is not just for a favoured few,
but for all who seek it.
Is there someone
among our friends or acquaintances
who at this present time
needs us to share
this Good News with them,
just as the early disciples
shared what they had discovered?**

A whole new way

Second Sunday after Epiphany. Year B

> Speak, your servant is listening. (1 Samuel 3.10 REB)
> Can anything good come from Nazareth? (John 1.46 REB)

Young and inexperienced,
Samuel's problem
was that he didn't recognize
the voice which was calling him;
but when he knew what he should do
his response was
immediate and whole-hearted:
'Speak, your servant is listening.'

Educated and sophisticated,
Nathaniel's problem
was that he had a very low opinion
of any who had not been brought up in Jerusalem,
especially if they came from the north of the country.

For Samuel
responding to the call of God
was a natural progression
from responding to the call of Eli.
For Nathaniel
responding to Jesus required
a whole new way of seeing things
a whole new way of judging things
a whole new way...

**We should like to think
that we were as ready as Samuel
to receive new truths;
but, if we are in fact
more like Nathaniel,
then, Father, lead us into
that whole new way
of thinking and behaving
which is a mark
of the citizens of your kingdom.**

A wedding to remember!

> As a bridegroom rejoices over the bride, so will your God rejoice over you. (Isaiah 62.5 REB)
>
> They are filled with the rich plenty of your house, and you give them to drink from the stream of your delights. (Psalm 36.8 REB)
>
> Everyone else serves the best wine first, and the poorer only when the guests have drunk freely; but you have kept the best wine till now. (John 2.10 REB)

What brought you, Lord, to that wedding at Cana?
You took time off from your mission
to be there,
but you don't appear to have given an address
or pronounced a special blessing.
All we are told is
that during the party,
when the wine had already been flowing freely
you provided a whole lot more.
Gallons of it!
It's as well that there weren't
any drink-driving laws in those days;
there would surely have been
quite a few merry people
in the village that night.

What's that you say, Lord?
You weren't taking time off,
it was all part of the mission!

Teach us, Lord, how to live
as your servants in the world
without draining the fun, the laughter
the exuberance and sheer joy
out of Christian living.
Teach us how to live for you with all our might
whilst at the same time being able to share
in the simple earthy pleasures of life.
Teach us how to be whole people.

So? What's the catch?

Third Sunday after Epiphany. Year A

> The Lord is my light and my salvation. (Psalm 27.1 REB)
> I appeal to you, my friends, in the name of our Lord Jesus Christ: agree among yourselves, and avoid divisions. (1 Corinthians 1.10 REB)
> Repent, for the kingdom of Heaven is upon you. (Matthew 4.17 REB)

Come!
You are invited to enter the kingdom of Heaven!
Don't worry about currency or passports,
and as for luggage,
the less you have the better;
the borders are open day and night,
and there are no restrictions!

So? What's the catch?

None!
There is no catch;
but the kingdom of a loving God
does require of its citizens
that they in turn should love,
beginning with one another,
and reaching out in ever widening circles.
Only so can the joys of the kingdom
be truly appreciated.

Lord of the kingdom,
forgive us, we pray,
all the hardness in our hearts,
all the resentments and stored injuries,
and anything else which hinders us
from growing as you would have us grow,
from growing in love.
Forgive us,
and bring about in us
such a radical change
that we may walk with joy
in the light which you shed on our way.

Call — and response

> A second time the word of the Lord came to Jonah: Go to the great city of Nineveh. (Jonah 3.1-2 REB)
> Come, follow me, and I will make you fishers of men. (Mark 1.17 REB)

Jonah
Jonah was a most reluctant prophet
who, when called to go to Nineveh,
set out as fast as he could in the opposite direction.
But the Lord bore with him
and called Jonah a second time.
So Jonah eventually went, grudgingly, to Nineveh,
the one bright spot, as he saw it, being
that he was to be the messenger of their doom.
Such was his hatred of Nineveh
that he preached as he had never preached before
and, to his amazement,
Nineveh repented and was spared.
Jonah was mad!
Patiently and gently,
God put to Jonah the question,
'Should I not show mercy to this people?
Should I not care for them
as much as I care for you?'

The Fishermen
It wasn't their first meeting,
they had already taken time from their fishing to be with Jesus
but now he was here,
confronting them during the working day.
'Come with me,' he said,
'I'm not just for high days and holidays,
this is for real —
O yes, you'll still need to earn a living,
but from now on your first job
is to serve the kingdom of God.'

Whenever and however your call comes,
may we be ready to hear,
and ready to give ourselves to your service,
whatever that may entail
and wherever it may lead.

Surely, not us?

Third Sunday after Epiphany. Year C

'Today', he said, 'in your hearing this text has come true.' (Luke 4.21 REB)
Now Christ's body is yourselves, each of you with a part to play in the whole.
(1 Corinthians 12.27 NJB)

From infancy
we have been trained to be spectators.
Before we could properly walk
we were sat in front of the television screen
to observe the antics of others.
Now we are older
we turn to the news bulletins
to learn what 'they' are doing
about the problems which face us.
We contribute to opinion polls
when we are asked,
but actually doing things is 'their' business;
we don't expect to be involved.

Of course we want to see
the coming of the Kingdom,
but,
well,
we have settled into a comfortable routine,
so we do hope that the coming of the kingdom
won't upset things too much.

We're sorry, Lord,
that we are liable to get too set in our ways
and need to be shaken up at times;
we do really want to be counted
as part of your people.
If you are calling for a change
in the way we think and act,
keep worrying us until we hear,
because we need you,
however slow we are to respond,
even when we complain about the demands
that are made upon us.

An acceptable offering

> What shall I bring when I come before the Lord? (Micah 6.6 REB)
> The folly of God is wiser than human wisdom, and the weakness of God
> stronger than human strength. (1 Corinthians 1.25 REB)
> Blessed are the poor in spirit... (Matthew 5.3ff REB)

'What should I bring?
What would be an appropriate gift,
fee, subscription,
or whatever the word is?
I'm prepared to put my hand in my pocket,
of course I am.
I don't expect the Lord's favour for nothing,
but I want to get it right.'

And here we come up against
the foolishness of God.
Pounds,
Dollars,
the Euro,
even gold
leave the Almighty
strangely unmoved.

**Heavenly Father,
We come, in our poverty.
We come, knowing that again and again
we have failed you.
We come asking you
to take us,
cleanse us,
renew us,
and then to show us
what it is that you really require;
that from the heart
we may bring
an acceptable offering
and serve you as we should.**

Simple, but direct

Fourth Sunday after Epiphany. Year B

> The fear of the Lord is the beginning of wisdom. (Psalm 111.10 REB)
> Unlike the scribes, he taught with a note of authority. (Mark 1.22 REB)
> 'Knowledge' inflates a man, whereas love builds him up. (1 Corinthians 8.1 REB)

He didn't argue from precedent;
he spoke simply,
directly,
and in plain language
which everybody could understand,
and he drew his illustrations from everyday life.
He spoke from the heart
to the heart
and as a friend to friends;
yet what he said
had an authenticity and authority
which his hearers immediately recognized.

His language was the language of love,
and the silences
when he listened to others
were equally eloquent.
None need fear to approach him
though all who came
had to be ready
to face the challenge to rise to new heights
and live their lives fully and selflessly,
at levels they had not previously thought possible.

Lord Jesus Christ,
may I be willing to listen for your word,
ready to take to heart what you would say to me,
and content to walk in the way you would have me go,
that in you, my life may find its meaning
and fulfil its purpose.

Not alone

Fourth Sunday after Epiphany. Year C

These words roused the whole congregation to fury. (Luke 4.28 REB)
Fear none of them, for I shall be with you to keep you safe. (Jeremiah 1.8 REB)

So you challenge the popular line,
you're alone;
and you do what you know you must do,
you're alone;
there's few will applaud you,
commend you or thank you,
so make no mistake,
you're alone — you're alone.

So a fire burns deep in your soul,
you're alone;
And you pour out the words in your heart,
you're alone,
there's few will applaud you,
commend you or thank you,
so make no mistake,
you're alone — you're alone.

Yet no one who searches for truth
is alone;
for they walk ever closer to God,
not alone;
there's one who goes with you
to strengthen, support you,
so make no mistake,
not alone, not alone.
(From *The Battle*)

Lord of the passing ages,
we thank you that succeeding generations
have been challenged by prophets
who declared unpopular truths
and refused to be intimidated
however bitter the opposition.
May we not be found wanting
if ever the day comes
when you will require similar bravery of us.

A different code

Fifth Sunday after Epiphany. Year A

Is not this the fast I require...? Is it not sharing your food with the hungry, taking the homeless poor into your house, clothing the naked when you meet them, and never evading a duty...? (Isaiah 58.6-7 REB)
Happy is he who fears the Lord, who finds deep delight in obeying his commandments. (Psalm 112.1 REB)
Like the lamp, you must shed light among your fellows. (Matthew 5.16 REB)

Who can live up to the searching demands
of the law of God?
So much easier to hide
within a thicket of rules and regulations
saying, 'All these have I kept —
I go to church on Sundays;
I don't drink,
smoke,
gamble,
swear or spit,
I don't...'

Yet Jesus,
who came to fulfil the law,
had little respect
for the forest of rules and regulations
which governed the lives
of the good religious people of his day.
He lived by a different code.

You have shown us the way, Lord;
give us the will,
the courage
and the strength
to follow in it
and to strive to live by the law
which requires of us that we not only
never knowingly wrong another,
but positively seek to do them good.
Teach us how to think ourselves
into another's situation,
to discover the joy of doing good by stealth
and of giving needed help
where none might have been expected.

Renewable resources

> But they that wait upon the Lord shall renew their strength; they shall mount up with wings as eagles; they shall run, and not be weary; and they shall walk, and not faint. (Isaiah 40.31 AV)
> Very early next morning he got up and went out. He went away to a remote spot and remained there in prayer. (Mark 1.35 REB)

Thanks be to God for the promise
of power to sustain us
in those sweet early days
of a new enterprise;
for the promise that in such an exciting time
we shall be able to find resources of strength
that will enable us to
'mount up with wings as eagles'.

Thanks be to God for the promise that,
when the time comes
to build upon
those foundations so enthusiastically laid,
we shall be able to find further resources;
enabling us to
'run and not be weary'.

Thanks be to God for the promise that,
when difficulties arise,
as they surely will,
and when what was begun with a light heart
now requires
a wearying attention to detail,
repetitive tasks,
slow consolidation;
when this,
the most demanding time of all arrives,
strength, if we seek it,
will again be given
and we shall be able to
'walk and not faint'.

Confronted by holiness

Fifth Sunday after Epiphany. Year C

> Holy, holy, holy! The Lord Almighty is holy! His glory fills the world.
> (Isaiah 6.3 GNB)
> I said, 'There is no hope for me! I am doomed because every word that passes
> my lips is sinful, and I live among a people whose every word is sinful.'
> (Isaiah 6.5 GNB)
> 'Go away from me, Lord! I am a sinful man.' (Luke 5.8 GNB)

Confronted by the holiness,
the 'otherness' of God,
Isaiah became aware, as never before, of the nature of sin;
became aware of the great gulf which exists
between the ways of the Almighty
and our ways.

In the cross of Jesus we see all too clearly
where self-righteousness, spite and hostility can lead,
but we also become aware of the evil done
through thoughtlessness, apathy and cowardice;
at the cross we are all involved,
none of us is free from guilt.

Yet in that same cross
we see how far God will go
to save us from our wilfulness
and all that makes up the darker side of our natures.
Holy and righteous, source of all integrity and truth;
our God is also a God of compassion, a God of love;
God bridges the gulf between us
and so from our own little, faltering love
we are able to bring to the Almighty
concerns laid on our own hearts.

**We thank you that from your holiness
flows a love which breaks through all barriers
and is always around and ahead of us.
Help us, and all for whom we pray,
to be ready and able
to receive the blessings
past all deserving
which we know you have for us,
through Jesus Christ, our Lord and Saviour.**

We have a choice

> Today I offer you the choice of life and good, or death and evil.
> (Deuteronomy 30.15 REB)
> Leave your gift where it is before the altar. First go and make your peace with
> your brother; then come back and offer your gift. (Matthew 5.24 REB)

Living is not automatic.
We all exist, but living is a matter of choice;
a matter of choosing
between
good and evil,
between
life and death.
Therefore choose life! (Deuteronomy 30.19)

And what is life
but the way of openness;
the way of
giving
and forgiving,
the way of
healing
and restoring?

You tell us, Lord, that reconciliation
has priority over worship;
but if we waited to put all wrongs to rights
we should never arrive.
So, now we're here,
if there is any bitterness in our hearts,
any stored anger or sense of hurt,
anything at all
which is a barrier
between us and another,
whoever they might be;
our prayer is
that you will release us from it,
that we may go from this place
determined, with your help,
to do all in our power
to repair any relationship which has gone astray.

Healing the inner sickness

Sixth Sunday after Epiphany. Year B

> Go and wash ... and you will be clean. (2 Kings 5.10 REB)
> He stretched out his hand, touched him, and said, 'I will; be clean.'
> (Mark 1.41 REB)

Two lepers!
The same outward symptoms of disease,
but two very different needs.

Naaman, though a leper,
was very conscious that he was a great man
and expected to be treated with deference.
Thus, when the healer
he had come so far to see
gave him no personal consultation,
merely sending out a servant with a message,
Naaman was furious.
Only when he overcame his pride sufficiently
to actually go and wash in the Jordan
was he healed.

The other leper was an outcast,
feared and shunned
because of his disease.
He was amazed that Jesus
should grasp him in a friendly embrace
as though his leprosy was no barrier.
Jesus first gave him back his self-respect
and then went on to heal the leprosy,
the two actions together
making the man whole.

We come to you, Lord, for healing;
but above all else we pray
that you will deal with any soul sickness,
be it false pride, self-despair,
or any other ill, even though at the moment
we may be unaware of our need.
If you will work this miracle in us
then, whatever bodily ills we may suffer,
we know we shall be whole.

It doesn't make sense — or does it?

> Happy is the one who does not take the counsel of the wicked for a guide.
> (Psalm 1.1 REB)
> If it is for this life only that Christ has given us hope, we of all people are most
> to be pitied. (1 Corinthians 15.19 REB)
> Turning to his disciples he began to speak... (Luke 6.20 REB)

'If you're poor,
hungry, crying your eyes out,
and getting the brush-off from everybody,
throw your hat in the air —
you've won the jackpot!

'But hard cheese if you've got a bit invested,
appreciate a good meal,
enjoy a laugh and are popular;
I wouldn't want to be in your shoes.
You'll soon be laughing on the other side of your face.'

Well, that's what Jesus said, isn't it?
Isn't it?
Yet he enjoyed a good meal and a drink —
one of the things his enemies pounced on.
He had a sense of humour
and for much of the time he was extremely popular.
So, what was he really saying?
It certainly makes you think.
Perhaps it was meant to.

**Lord, your teaching is a bit 'iffy' at times
and we're not always sure what you were getting at;
but you do make us very uneasy
about our attitudes to wealth and poverty,
to success and failure.
Is that the point?
Is it that
where your teaching
is hardest to follow
we are meant to wrestle with it?
Is that how we are to come
to a deeper understanding of your ways?**

37

Lord, reshape the lives we offer

Seventh Sunday after Epiphany. Year A

You must be holy ... You must love your neighbour as yourself. I am the Lord.
(Leviticus 19.2,18 REB)
Do you not realize that you are a temple of God with the Spirit of God living in
you? (1 Corinthians 3.16 NJB)
There must be no limit to your goodness, as your heavenly Father's goodness
knows no bounds. (Matthew 5.48 REB)

Lord, reshape the lives we offer,
when we stumble, be our guide;
heal our poverty of spirit,
strike our arrogance and pride;
let your love possess, remould us,
till you reign and self has died.

When you call us into action
may we listen and obey;
where the saints of old have trodden
may we follow in that way;
fight in this our generation
battles that are ours today.

Stir in us a holy anger
when your people are oppressed;
may we show a Christlike passion
for the poor and dispossessed,
for the weak and disadvantaged
give ourselves, and give our best.

Make us, Lord, a pilgrim people
striking camp and moving on;
freed from bondage to tradition
and the days that long have gone,
ever ready for new duties
in the steps of Christ your Son.
(From *Cuthbert*)

'I am about to do something new'

> Stop dwelling on past events and brooding over days gone by. I am about to do something new. (Isaiah 43.18-19 REB)
> All the promises of God have their Yes in him [Christ Jesus].
> (2 Corinthians 1.20 REB)
> Your sins are forgiven. (Mark 2.5 REB)

A dying church?
A world that has outgrown God?
A life where we are on our own
and the outlook is bleak?
Isaiah had heard it all;
but he had also heard the Lord
speaking in his heart
and saying,
'I am about to do something new'.

**Lord, when we come to worship,
save us from
giving way to nostalgia,
recalling times long past,
and behaving as though we were
attending a memorial service.
Remind us, should we need reminding,
that you are a risen, living Christ,
who meets us
and calls us to service
in the contemporary world.
When we come, may we,
in fellowship one with another,
be listening together
for your word to us.
May we expect to be challenged,
expect to be shaken out of complacency,
and be ready to be led
into whatever fresh adventures
you may have for us.**

A chance for revenge

Seventh Sunday after Epiphany. Year C

I am your brother Joseph ... I can take care of you. (Genesis 45.4,11 GNB)
Trust in the Lord and do good. (Psalm 37.3 GNB)
Love your enemies, do good to those who hate you. (Luke 6.27 GNB)

Joseph
'They've come from Canaan;
the famine has reached as far as that?'
Outwardly I was in control, my voice was steady,
but inwardly I was in turmoil.
Canaan, the land of my happy childhood.
Canaan, the land I had left,
sold by my brothers into slavery
after interminable hours in a stinking pit.

Yes, I could see them there,
my brothers,
rather, half-brothers, sons of Leah,
but not Benjamin, not my own mother's other son.
They did not recognize me,
why should they,
they hardly raised their eyes?
Now they were in my power.
Three days I let them stew in prison, accused of spying,
before I sent them back
with the grain they sought
and their money returned,
though in such a way as to cause them some anxiety.
When they came again
I had further tricks to play...

But, I cannot continue in this way,
whatever the past
they are my brothers —
they are in need —
and I have means...

'Come nearer,
raise your eyes and look at me:
I am your brother Joseph ... I can take care of you.'

A little matter of money

> Now stewards are required to show themselves trustworthy.
> (1 Corinthians 4.2 REB)
> You cannot serve God and Money ... Surely life is more than food, the body more
> than clothes. (Matthew 6.24-25 REB)

There's nothing wrong with money,
why should there be?
Money is a tool
and a very useful tool at that.
The only question,
as with all tools,
is what use I make of it.

Of course,
being a very powerful tool,
money is dangerous.
I can easily become obsessed with money,
set it up as an idol,
and worship it.
But if I can resist that temptation,
and it can be a very great temptation,
I know that,
handled with care,
money can do much good.

**Help us, we pray,
to grow in understanding
of what it is that you require of your stewards.
Grant us the will and the strength
to handle responsibly
whatever wealth may come into our hands.
Save us from either hoarding
or wasting money
and show us how to use
whatever we have,
be it little or much,
wisely and generously
as befits your servants.**

Prayer for a troubled world

Eighth Sunday after Epiphany. Year B

> I will ... make Trouble Valley a door of hope. (Hosea 2.15 GNB)
> People who are well do not need a doctor, but only those who are sick.
> (Mark 2.17 GNB)

We live in a troubled world, Lord,
yet a world in which you have lived a human life
and in which you are still present,
sharing its pains and sorrows,
and we believe that you call us to reflect
your own loving concern in our prayers.

We pray for peace.
The spotlight moves from one area of conflict to another.
We hear the news, we see the pictures,
but our minds cannot comprehend the scale
of the misery and the suffering of those involved;
yet we lift them up in the confidence
that every single soul is dear to you.

We pray for those in areas devastated by natural disasters —
flood, drought, earthquake, storm, volcanic eruption;
and for those eking out a living in marginal lands,
or who have become penniless squatters
in the earth's great cities.

We pray for women in traditions
which deny them opportunities open to men
and for all, men, women, children, whose lives are stunted
because of prejudice, exploitation or oppression.

Loving Saviour, you give yourself to us
holding nothing back;
let your love so flood our hearts
that we ourselves may be
messengers of peace,
helpers of the poor,
comforters of the distressed
and workers for justice,
through your grace and for your sake.

Always a living Word

> So it is with my word issuing from my mouth; it will not return to me empty.
> (Isaiah 55.11 REB)
> Everyone who comes to me and hears my words and acts on them ... is like a
> man building a house, who dug deep and laid the foundations on rock.
> (Luke 6.47-48 REB)

We come to you,
our God and Father,
because you are the same
from generation to generation.
Yet, when we listen,
really listen,
there is always
something new,
something surprising,
something startling
in what you are saying to us.
At times we are shaken,
at times we are hurt,
yet we know we must still listen,
and listening
we learn that your Word
is always a living Word,
and that the work
to which you call us
is always a contemporary task.

**Living Lord Jesus,
as we go out to proclaim your Good News
— through all the differences of emphasis
— through all the differences of presentation
— whether in cathedral or kitchen;
let our mouths speak your words,
and let our lives reflect your life,
that your name may be glorified
and the world may believe.**

43

A glimpse of a greater reality

Last Sunday after Epiphany. Year A

> The glory of the Lord rested on Mount Sinai, and the cloud covered the mountain.
> (Exodus 24.16 REB)
> Worship the Lord with reverence; tremble, and pay glad homage to the king.
> (Psalm 2.11 REB)
> Then Jesus came up to them, touched them, and said, 'Stand up; do not be afraid.'
> (Matthew 17.7 REB)

Before the beginning —
Yet, could there be anything before the beginning?
I wrestle with words, with images,
but it is past my imagining;
all I can write is —
Before the beginning — God!

You breathed the Word of creation and time began;
the sands began to run through the glass —
But is time finite?
Just one more unanswered question —
You conceived both the vastness of space
and the intricacy of the microscopic particle.
In the stillness, in awe and wonder, I worship
not what I know, but that which is beyond my knowing;
not what I see, but that which is hidden from my sight;
not what I can express in words,
but that which is inexpressible.

Beyond the reach of investigative journalism;
not to be captured by the camera's eye;
impervious to our most advanced technology;
your glory, your 'otherness'
dazzles, even through the protective cloud.

Holy and righteous God,
God of blinding glory,
your ways are far removed from our ways
and yet in Jesus you say to us,
'Do not be afraid,
I accept you just as you are.
Come, be my people
and I will be your God.'
Father, we come.

Morning on the mountain

Last Sunday after Epiphany. Year B

> And suddenly there appeared a chariot of fire and horses of fire, which separated them from one another, and Elijah was carried up to heaven in a whirlwind. (2 Kings 2.11 REB)
> The light which is knowledge of the glory of God in the face of Jesus Christ. (2 Corinthians 4.6 REB)
> They saw Elijah appear and Moses with him, talking with Jesus ... they were so terrified. (Mark 9.4,6 REB)

A disciple
We set out at dawn
and soon we were climbing the mountainside.
When we reached the place we held back a little
that he might pray alone.
All was still...

Suddenly, dazzled, confused, terrified,
we were in a different world.
Elijah was with him,
Elijah who had defied all the priests of Baal
and called down fire from heaven to consume his sacrifice.
And Moses, whom God used
to lead our people out of Egypt and give the law.
And Jesus himself was changed, was transfigured.
We babbled something, but it was meaningless
and then cloud covered us and we heard the voice:
'This is my beloved Son; listen to him'.

Then we were back to our stumbling discipleship,
our everyday world and our many failures,
but held, as ever, in his love.

Holy and glorious God,
you are far beyond the reach of our understanding,
yet we would listen to and follow your Son,
our Lord Jesus Christ.
Grant us constancy as we seek to serve him,
forgive our many failures,
and enfold us, we pray, in his salvation
that, through his sacrifice,
we may at the last be able to enter into your presence.

Touched by the glory

Last Sunday after Epiphany. Year C

His face shone because he had been talking with the Lord. (Exodus 34.29 REB)
And because for us there is no veil over the face, we all see as in a mirror the glory of the Lord. (2 Corinthians 3.18 REB)
The appearance of his face changed and his clothes became dazzling white. (Luke 9.29 REB)

They looked ... *different!*
They had been with God
and were reflecting something of his glory.
The change was startling.

Perhaps that's how it should always be,
that we should look different.
Maybe not radiant like Moses,
or like our Lord looked on this occasion;
not more handsome
or more beautiful
(no good expecting that!)
but —
more alive, more aware,
more understanding, more caring
more loving...
different!

**God of the past,
God of the future,
God of the now;
we both long and fear
to know more of your glory.
We long for you
as the source of all that is lovely and true;
yet we fear that your presence
will illumine the darkest corners of our souls,
forcing us to know ourselves as we really are.
Yet come, Lord,
come, despite our fears;
show us as much of your glory as we can bear,
that we may be changed
and some spark of that glory
be reflected through our own living.**

O Lord, forgive

> Rend your hearts and not your garments. (Joel 2.13 REB)
> Wash away all my iniquity and cleanse me from my sin. (Psalm 51.2 REB)
> We implore you in Christ's name, be reconciled to God! (2 Corinthians 5.20 REB)

O Lord, forgive, O Lord, forgive,
O Jesus, Lord, forgive.
We trusted, yet we trusted not,
we feared to follow where you led;
we trusted, yet we trusted not
enough to tread the way you tread.
We could not have a better friend
and yet we failed you at the end.

We saw you multiply the bread
and turn the water into wine;
yet when you rode upon an ass
we failed to understand the sign.
We sought a kingdom in the sky
and missed it as it passed us by.
O Lord, forgive, O Lord, forgive,
O Jesus, Lord, forgive.

O living Christ, forgive me now
for you were crucified for me.
The bonds of selfishness and pride,
break through them all and set me free.
O Saviour, in your risen might
bring me from darkness into light.
O Lord, forgive, O Lord, forgive,
O Jesus, Lord, forgive.
(From *Upside Down And Inside Out*)

Lord, let me not be blind to my sins.
May I know where I am weak
that I may look to you for strength.
May I know where I have done wrong
that I may look to you to help me
to put wrong to rights.
May I recognize when I am astray,
that I may look to you to lead me
back into the way of life.

You will be like God

First Sunday in Lent. Year A

> You will be like God himself, knowing both good and evil. (Genesis 3.5 REB)

He was most friendly,
so easy to get along with,
and it sounded very reasonable.
'You have nothing to fear,' he said,
'making choices is part of the process of growing up,
and you mustn't be held back
by old-fashioned ideas of morality.
Undreamed-of opportunities lie ahead of you
so grasp them while you can.
Don't keep looking over your shoulder
and talking about God;
those days of dependence have gone.
It's time to make your own way,
time to be your own God.'

— So the holocaust.
— So Hiroshima and Nagasaki.
— So the search for ever more deadly
            weapons of destruction.
— So unmanageable burdens of debt
            heaped on the poorest nations.
— So global warming.
— So ethnic cleansing...

'You will be like God himself,' he said,
'knowing both good and evil.
You have nothing to fear'.

Lord, we cannot turn back the clock,
and change the course of history;
but we could learn from the past.
In your mercy, forgive our arrogance
and teach us the humility
we so desperately need
if we are to handle properly your precious gifts
which can either enrich or destroy us all.
You alone can lead us to a full and satisfying life.
You alone are God.

We live by faith

> For all generations to come, this is the sign which I am giving of the covenant between myself and you and all living creatures. (Genesis 9.12 REB)
> Lead me by your faithfulness and teach me, for you are God my saviour. (Psalm 25.5 REB)
> The time has arrived; the kingdom of God is upon you. Repent, and believe the gospel. (Mark 1.15 REB)

After seemingly endless rain
and unprecedented flooding,
the sun shone again
and the sight of the delicate,
shimmering rainbow
brought promise and hope.

When the brutal reality of the cross
mocked the good news of the Kingdom
and all seemed lost,
Christ rose from the dead!
The end became the beginning
and the cross itself became a sign of hope.

The kingdom of God is upon you.
Repent, and believe the gospel!

Rainbow God!
Resurrection God!
We live in the faith
that you fulfil your promises
and deal with us beyond all deserving.
Help us when our skies are dark
to wait expectantly for the rainbow,
and in the face of death
to have confident hope in the resurrection.

The time to beware

First Sunday in Lent. Year C

> When he calls to me, I shall answer. (Psalm 91.15 REB)
> Everyone who calls on the name of the Lord will be saved. (Romans 10.13 REB)
> Led by the Spirit and tempted by the devil. (Luke 4.1 REB)

We come to you
confessing our sins.
> *'This, Lord, I have done*
> *which I should not have done,*
> *and this which I should have done*
> *I have failed to do.*
> *I am sorry, I will try to put things right.*
> *Please forgive me.'*

But thinking on the temptations
which confronted Jesus in the wilderness,
we realize that this is the easy part —
admitting the sins we recognize;
the hard part is facing up to the sins
we don't even recognize as sins.

If Jesus needed to wrestle with all his might
to distinguish truth from falsehood
when the devil came as an angel of light
saying, 'This is the way to establish the kingdom';
how much more must we be aware
of the need to distinguish in our own lives
which is of the Spirit
and which of the adversary.

Lord, if you had to struggle with the tempter
what hope would I have, except you helped me?
Save me from being confident
that I can always know right from wrong,
especially when I am making judgments
on the actions of others.
Let me never fear to acknowledge
my weakness and my uncertainties
and help me to be always on my guard
lest my strongest convictions be moulded
by the enemy rather than by you.

He came by night

> One of the Pharisees, called Nicodemus, a member of the Jewish Council, came
> to Jesus by night. (John 3.1 REB).

Nicodemus
Something died in me that night.
The Council were already discussing
how they might best be rid of him,
but I wanted to meet the man,
to talk with him myself.
Asking where he might be found,
I slipped round quietly, after dark;
I had barely finished the introductory courtesies
when he said that I needed to forget
all I had ever learned and start afresh —
he used the term 'be born again'.
He caught me off my guard.
I certainly hadn't expected this,
and yet something drew me to him,
some strange inner authority
which never left him
even when he was condemned
and crucified.

Those days are now long gone,
yet by the mercy of God
he is much closer to me now
than he was then.
Something died in me that night
and something new,
something precious and enduring was born.

May my mind be open to fresh revelation
and to new understandings of ancient truth.
May my heart be as ready to trust my God
as a newborn child is to trust a loving parent.
May I, unfettered by anything in the past,
be ready to grasp and accept
whatever the future may hold for me.
May I continue to be 'born again'.

When hope seems hopeless

Second Sunday in Lent. Year B

> I shall make you father of many nations. (Genesis 17.5 REB)
> He has not scorned him who is downtrodden. (Psalm 22.24 REB)
> When hope seemed hopeless, his faith was such that he became
> 'father of many nations'. (Romans 4.18 REB)
> Whoever wants to save his life will lose it, but whoever loses his life for my sake
> and for the gospel's will save it. (Mark 8.35 REB)

It was many years
since they had first set out from Ur.
Now Abraham and Sarah were old,
still nomads in the land of Canaan
and still without a son.
Though they were never to own more than a burial place
in the promised land
they travelled in faith,
trusting that their pilgrimage would find its fulfilment
long after their bodies had returned to the dust.

The call to become pilgrims,
to seek an eternal kingdom,
to be ready to lose one's life to save it,
is an enigma,
until we remember the ways in which we see
God at work in human history;
remember that the Church is founded
on a death and a resurrection.

The kingdom of God
is built brick by brick
of 'failures',
of glorious 'failures'.
It is not 'success' that is valued in the kingdom,
not success, but faithfulness.

**Lord, so hold us
that even in darkest days
we may lose neither our faith
in your promises,
nor our awareness
that we are supported by your love.**

The reality of evil

> Abram fell into a trance and great and fearful darkness came over him.
> (Genesis 15.12 REB)
> The Lord is my light and my salvation; whom should I fear? (Psalm 27.1 REB)
> There are many whose way of life makes them enemies of the cross of Christ.
> (Philippians 3.18 REB)
> O Jerusalem, Jerusalem, city that murders the prophets and stones the
> messengers sent to her! (Luke 13.34 REB)

A 'fearful darkness' envelops Abram
even as he contemplates
the promises of God.

Paul writes with great affection
to a community he loves,
yet he is burdened by the fact
that even within that community
there are those whose ways,
despite all professions of faith,
make them 'enemies of Christ'.

Jesus approaches the holy city, Jerusalem,
as the climax of his mission draws near,
knowing even as he travels
that he will be rejected and killed.

There is no escaping the reality or the power of evil.

'Save us from the time of trial and deliver us from evil.
For the kingdom, the power, and the glory are yours, now and for ever.'

If ever the fearful, penetrating darkness of evil
should threaten to engulf me,
draining energy, sapping willpower,
making my spirit desolate;
even though it seems I have lost my hold on you
do not you, my God, lose hold of me.
Bring me safely, I pray, through to the light again;
in the name of him who met evil head on,
was slain, and rose again;
Jesus Christ, our Lord and Saviour.

Water of life

Third Sunday in Lent. Year A

Strike the rock; water will pour out of it. (Exodus 17.6 REB)
Christ died for us while we were yet sinners. (Romans 5.8 REB)
The water that I shall give will be a spring of water within him, welling up
and bringing eternal life. (John 4.14 REB)

Strike the rock,
dig the well,
build the dam —
but first survey the ground,
test the technology,
consider the impact on the environment
and then the thirsty may indeed drink
and the hungry eat and be satisfied.

But what of us
who eat and are not satisfied,
who live in comfort
and yet are not at ease?
We have eagerly grasped
the world's riches
and found them strangely unsatisfying.
Is there really something we have missed?
Something more desirable?
Something more lasting?

Heavenly Father,
whenever we are in danger
of being possessed
by the selfish materialism of our time,
remind us again that your way,
the way that enables us
to drink the enduring water of life,
is a way of loving self-giving,
which calls us to help satisfy
the hunger and thirst
of others of your children
with material needs far greater than our own.

Cleaning up the act

> I am the Lord your God ... You must have no other god besides me.
> (Exodus 20.2-3 REB)
> The law of the Lord is perfect and revives the soul. (Psalm 19.7 REB)
> God has made the wisdom of this world look foolish! (1 Corinthians 1.20 REB)
> Take all this out of here and stop using my Father's house as a market.
> (John 2.16 NJB)

Lord, in the complexity of the modern world
we couldn't exist without our banks,
our financial institutions,
our 'money-changers'.
We need them,
just as we need the markets
which make possible
the exchange of the goods and services
upon which our lives depend.

We know there are many faults
in our economic system
and that the gulf between rich and poor
is far too great;
but without our financiers and our merchants
we should have chaos.

Are you telling us,
not so much that these things are wrong,
as that we have done wrong
in idolizing wealth
and the institutions and systems which create it?
That our lives are the poorer
because we have given to wealth
the place which belongs only to you?

Teach us to value money
for what may be achieved by using it wisely;
teach us to value the market as a means of bringing
goods and services where they are needed;
but above all,
teach us to handle the earth's riches
with reverence and the awareness
that they are given for us all.

Accident in Siloam

Third Sunday in Lent. Year C

Let the wicked abandon their ways and the evil their thoughts: let them return
to the Lord, who will take pity on them, and to our God, for he will
freely forgive. (Isaiah 55.7 REB)
Or the eighteen people who were killed when the tower fell on them at
Siloam—do you imagine they must have been more guilty than all the other
people living in Jerusalem? (Luke 13.4 REB)

But why did the tower in Siloam fall?
Was it a matter of poor foundations,
an error in design,
shoddy materials?
Was it the fault of
the builder,
the architect,
the merchant who supplied the bricks and mortar?
Was it something which couldn't have been anticipated
or a disaster waiting to happen?

And who were the unfortunate eighteen killed?
Workmen,
women out shopping,
children on a school outing?

Creator God, we tell ourselves
that your world would be much simpler to understand
if the good were always rewarded
and unpleasant things happened only to the guilty;
but then we remember the uncomfortable fact
that we are all guilty,
that we all offend against your ways.
Forgive us, we pray,
both our evil thoughts and our sinful deeds,
and strengthen our compassion
for all who suffer,
whatever the reason for their suffering.

Wilful blindness

Fourth Sunday in Lent. Year A

Learn to judge for yourselves what is pleasing to the Lord. (Ephesians 5.10 REB)
It is for judgment that I have come into this world—to give sight to the sightless
and to make blind those who see. (John 9.39 REB)

A man born blind
Blind I might have been,
but I could hear them talking about me
as though I was a block of wood or a lump of stone.
'Whose fault is it that this man was born blind?'
As if it mattered whose fault it was.
I was cursed with blindness
and nothing was going to change that.

Then, there was a voice I hadn't heard before,
something was being laid on my eyes
and that same voice told me to go and wash them.
So I went — and washed — and — yes, I could see!

It's a strange old world though;
instead of congratulations I was met with complaints.
It seems my sight had been restored in the wrong way,
by the wrong man, on the wrong day.
Rules had been broken!
Holy law ignored!
Well, I didn't know anything about all that,
but one thing I knew for sure
and I didn't mind telling them:
Once I was blind and now I can see!

For him the glory of the Lord had been revealed.
The others remained blind.

Deliver us, O God, from bondage to tradition;
save us from blind eyes and closed minds.
Grant us the humility to welcome
new truths, new tasks,
new ways of seeing things,
that we may recognize your presence,
especially when you may be
challenging us to think afresh
about what your service requires of us today.

To heal the sickness of our souls

Fourth Sunday in Lent. Year B

So Moses made a bronze serpent and erected it as a standard, in order that
anyone bitten by a snake could look at the bronze serpent and recover.
(Numbers 21.9 REB)
Just as Moses lifted up the serpent in the wilderness, so the Son of Man must
be lifted up, in order that everyone who has faith may in him have eternal life.
(John 3.14-15 REB)

It was snakebite that caused Moses
to raise the serpent in the wilderness;
but it was the venom
of a far more deadly snake
which lifted Christ upon the cross
to bear the weight
of the sins and sorrows of humanity.

*God so loved the world that he gave his only Son, that everyone who has faith in him may
not perish but have eternal life. It was not to judge the world that God sent his Son into
the world, but that through him the world might be saved. (John 3.16-17 REB)*

Father God, we thank you
that in the living and dying
of our Lord Jesus Christ
you have made your nature known to us;
that what he was in a human life
you are eternally.
We thank you
that while you are a righteous God
you are also a God of love,
compassion, understanding and forgiveness;
that you are ever reaching out
to save us from ourselves.
Continue your healing work in us, we pray;
strengthen our faith
and draw us ever closer to yourself;
that, knowing ourselves held secure
in a love which will never fail us,
we may reflect some of that love to others
through our daily living in the world,
your world,
the world Christ died to save.

Two homecomings

> Happy is he whose offence is forgiven, whose sin is blotted out! (Psalm 32.1 REB)
> God was in Christ reconciling the world to himself, no longer holding
> people's misdeeds against them, and has entrusted us with the message
> of reconciliation. (2 Corinthians 5.19 REB)
> There was once a man who had two sons. (Luke 15.11 REB)

An old family servant
I kept out of the way when I saw he was back.
He'd been on a business trip,
so the first he knew of his brother coming home
was seeing the party in full swing
and the fatted calf on the barbecue.
And when he learned
the lad had come back penniless —
well, that was the last straw.
He was mad!
And he'd got a point, don't you think?
He'd been more or less running the business
for the last few years
and to see all that excitement
about the one who'd nearly ruined it...
To make matters worse,
he never was a one for parties.
He's a decent fellow, good to work for,
a bit set in his ways, but straight as a die.

The younger brother?
A charmer, but irresponsible.
He'd always been a bit of a handful
and it was a tidy sum of money
he'd gone off with and squandered.

How did it all finish, d'you say?
Well, I don't rightly know;
I took another job and moved away.
But I reckon the elder one had enough of his father in him
to make him come round eventually.
I don't think he would ever have
really approved of his younger brother,
but I guess he came to accept him as he was —
for his father's sake.

Calling the dead to life

Fifth Sunday in Lent. Year A

> O man, can these bones live? (Ezekiel 37.3 REB)
> In the Lord is love unfailing, and great is his power to deliver. (Psalm 130.7 REB)
> The God who raised Christ Jesus from the dead will also give new life to your mortal bodies through his indwelling Spirit. (Romans 8.11 REB)
> Then he raised his voice in a great cry: 'Lazarus, come out.' (John 11.43 REB)

Once the 'people of God',
now they were dead,
so very dead;
like the weathered bones of warriors
strewn on an ancient battlefield.
Yet the prophet,
believing that with God all things are possible,
answers the call to preach
even to dry bones —
and the bones begin to live.

Lazarus was dead
and four days in his tomb
when Jesus came.
Even those who had loved him dearly
were reluctant to roll back the stone,
Yet Jesus —
the resurrection and the life —
calls to him in a great cry,
and Lazarus stumbles out to the light,
a man restored to life again.

Lord, except for the love which cherishes us
we should be lost:
except for the mercy which forgives us
we would stand condemned;
except for the life which seeks us
we should be dead:
but through your total giving of yourself
we are found, forgiven, and restored to life.
Thanks be to God.

Renewal

> I shall set my law within them, writing it on their hearts; I shall be their God, and they will be my people. (Jeremiah 31.33 REB)
> Now my soul is in turmoil, and what am I to say? 'Father, save me from this hour'? No, it was for this that I came to this hour. Father, glorify your name. (John 12.27-28 REB)

When I mark up the balance sheet of my daily living,
even though I cheat a little,
even though I am somewhat economical with the truth,
it still comes out badly on the wrong side.
The more I give myself to self-examination,
the less I can find to be pleased about.
Even when I appear to have done quite well
there remains a nagging question
about mixed motives,
which I cannot completely silence.
I know that I cannot get things straight by myself,
I need God;
I have always needed God,
and I always will.

Create in me a clean heart, O God; and renew a right spirit within me. Cast me not away from thy presence; and take not thy holy spirit from me. Restore unto me the joy of thy salvation; and uphold me with thy free spirit. (Psalm 51.10-12 AV.)

**Help me now, Heavenly Father,
that I may come with reverence
as I seek your presence;
with wonder
as I recall again your love and compassion,
and with thanksgiving
for the many blessings
I have received throughout my life.
May I go out this day
with my trust in you strengthened,
my love rekindled
and my purpose to serve you renewed
through Jesus Christ my Lord.**

A wildly extravagant gesture

Fifth Sunday in Lent. Year C

Stop dwelling on past events and brooding over days gone by. I am about
to do something new; this moment it will unfold. Can you not perceive it?
(Isaiah 43.18-19 REB)
We were like people renewed in health. Our mouths were full of laughter
(Psalm 126.1-2 REB)
I count everything sheer loss, far outweighed by the gain of knowing
Christ Jesus my Lord. (Philippians 3.8 REB)
Could not this perfume have been sold? (John 12.5 REB)

Paul would have understood
the extravagance of love
expressed in the anointing of Jesus;
but Paul's dramatic conversion was yet to come,
and the action must have sent shock waves
around the room that night.
Of course the perfume could have been sold,
and for a very good price.
It might have fetched
as much as a labourer
could earn in a year.
Judas voiced the disquiet,
but he would have only been putting into words
the unease which others were feeling.
Was this not a terrible waste of resources?

Almighty God,
we know that churches, charities, aid organizations,
all need to be able to give an account of their stewardship;
just as individually we have a responsibility
to use our own resources wisely
and with a proper concern
for what your service requires of us.
But help us also to recognize those times
when love requires a different yardstick,
and let there be a warmth about all our giving
and our understanding of the actions of others,
for the sake of Jesus Christ our Lord
who gave his all for us,
holding nothing back.

Palm Sunday religion

Sixth Sunday in Lent. Liturgy of the Palms. Years A, B & C

Hosanna to the Son of David! Blessed is he who comes in the name of the Lord!
Hosanna in the heavens!
(Matthew 21.9 REB. cf Mark 11. 9-10; Luke 19.38; John 12.13)

Palm Sunday religion can be a very shallow thing.
> 'Hosanna to the Son of David!
> Ride on, ride on, we're right behind you;
> don't forget us when the share-out comes.'

Palm Sunday religion can be an all-too-easy expectation
that God will wave a magic wand
and solve all our problems;
but that isn't the way of things.

Jesus entering Jerusalem on an ass
cannot be separated from
Jesus leaving Jerusalem carrying a cross.

True religion begins
when we realize that, humanly speaking,
there isn't going to be any share-out.
True religion starts from the knowledge
that we shall have to go on living with our problems,
holding on to the faith
that God is facing them with us,
even when we feel abandoned,
even when we're in the mire up to our necks.

When we cry out to God
for justice for the oppressed
we are met with the reply,
'I have stripped myself of the power to do these things
that you might be free.
I am the hungry, the homeless, the unemployed,
the dispossessed, the alien, the inarticulate.
If the hungry are to be fed, the helpless championed,
the ignorant taught, the alien welcomed;
you must be my hands, my voice.'

This is what it is to be of the kingdom,
not cheering on the sidelines,
but involved in the rough and tumble
of serving a needy world.

The coming of the King

Here is your King. (Matthew 21.5 REB. cf Mark 11.10, Luke 19.38 & John 12.13)

When Jesus rode into Jerusalem
to be welcomed as God's promised Messiah,
his disciples must surely have found
all their fears and doubts evaporating
in the warmth of that reception
and the hope that the kingdom was now at hand.
Then came days of mounting tension;
fears returned, hopes were cast down;
brutally swiftly the scene changed,
Jesus was betrayed, arrested
and crucified.

From the heights
they were plunged into the depths.
It was only when they had reached rock bottom,
all hope gone,
that they discovered, to their amazement,
that the kingdom had indeed come
and come in a way
they could never possibly have imagined.
In the days that followed
it drew from them a strength and courage
which they never knew they had,
and gave them joy
beyond anything they had previously experienced.

**We should have thought it folly, Lord,
to ride, unguarded into Jerusalem
knowing that rejection and death lay ahead;
leaving all the hopes of your mission
in the hands of a ragbag group of followers.
And yet we see that this folly
was wiser than all our wisdom.
Lord, help us to let go of whatever hinders us
from seeing things from your perspective
and help us to recognize the signs
that show your kingdom
is even now actively at work in our midst.**

Another man's load

Sixth Sunday in Lent. Liturgy of the Passion. Years A, B & C

As they led him away to execution they took hold of a man called Simon, from Cyrene, on his way in from the country; putting the cross on his back they made him carry it behind Jesus. (Luke 23.26 REB. cf Matthew 27.32; Mark 15.21)

Another man's load, I was lumbered,
stuck with another man's load;
nobody wanting to know a thing
as I stumbled along the road.
I cursed the fate that clobbers a man
and then — how could it be? —
I looked straight into the other man's face;
it was full of pity for me.

Another man's pain, I was crying,
racked with another man's grief;
landed in trouble up to the neck,
never a hope of relief.
Why in the hell should they pick on me
to drink of this bitter vine?
Then I looked straight into the other man's face;
he was bearing pain that was mine.

Another man's cross, I was reeling
with another man's cross on my back;
singled out for the gruesome load,
staggering, ready to crack;
and all my muscles shrieked with pain
'twas the ghastliest road ever trod,
then I looked straight into the other man's face
and the eyes were the eyes of God.
(From *One Friday in Eternity*)

This was a hard thing, Lord, for Simon,
to be suddenly forced to share the burden
of your humiliation, pain and sorrows.
This was a very hard thing
and always will be;
yet if ever such a burden should be laid upon me
give me courage and strength to accept it
and to carry it willingly for your sake.

More than a man can do

Sixth Sunday in Lent. Liturgy of the Passion. Years A, B & C

> When the centurion who was standing opposite him saw how he died, he said,
> 'This man must have been a son of God.'
> (Mark 15.39 REB. cf Matthew 27.54; Luke 23.47)

After the crucifixion the Centurion present addresses Mary

CENTURION Are you his mother, Ma'am?
My sympathy.
You'll reckon me a hardened old soldier,
maybe I am.
I'm what fifteen years in the service of the Empire
has made me;
but I still don't like this sort of duty
and I don't mind saying so,
and as far as today's business goes,
I'll be as glad as the rawest recruit
to get drunk tonight and forget it.
By all accounts he meant well, Ma'am,
but it's not enough to mean well;
if your ideas are likely to shake the system
you'll be crucified along with thugs and murderers
for all your good intentions.
There's plenty of things I'd like to see changed, plenty.
But it's no good dreaming of a better world
until somebody finds an answer to the cross
and I don't think that's going to come in our time.
I reckon it's more than a man can do, Ma'am,
more than a man can do.
(From *Out Of This world*)

If ever we begin to believe
that the forces of evil are too great for us
and are tempted to give up the struggle,
saying that there is nothing we can do;
remind us again that you are a God
who can turn defeat into victory
and who confronts death itself with resurrection.

An example to be followed

> I have set you an example: you are to do as I have done for you. (John 13.15 REB)

He washed their feet,
for none of his disciples had been willing
to take up the basin and towel when they arrived.
When he had finished, he said to them,
'I have given you an example',
but that applied not merely to the feet washing,
but to the whole of the time he had been with them.

The example he had given
was of an independent and courageous mind
which never for a moment forgot
that the whole meaning and purpose of his existence
was to give glory to God.

And he showed that giving glory to God
was an exciting adventure.
He often broke the rules
which good religious people cherished and lived by;
but when he broke them
it was that he might reach out
to other men or women whose lives were
for one reason or another in a mess.

He challenged the assumption
that success in life is a matter of trying to climb higher
up the slippery pole;
and he lived as he died,
for the sake of others.

Lord, we would follow your example.
We know we shan't always get it right
even when we are really trying;
and so our prayer is
that, when we do go astray,
you will make us aware of our failures
and, of your mercy, bring us back into the way.

Bread broken for the world

Holy Thursday. Years A, B & C

> For every time you eat this bread and drink the cup, you proclaim the death of the Lord, until he comes. (1 Corinthians 11.26 REB)

I cannot proclaim the death of the Lord in isolation.
It is wonderful to think that Christ died for me, personally,
but he did not die for me exclusively.
Christ died for my sisters and brothers
the whole world over,
for the whole human race.
He invites each and every one of us
to become part of his body
and so part of one another,
and he says to each and to all of us,
'This is the way that others shall know you for my disciples,
that you love one another.'

We gather at his table conscious of Christ's invitation.
We also come conscious of sin,
conscious of our need for forgiveness.
Yet forgiveness depends on the will to put wrongs to right,
so if there is someone I couldn't care less about
I'd better be making a little more effort
to get on terms with them.
I cannot be in true fellowship with my Lord
if I am divided from my fellows
by indifference, snobbery, theological correctness,
or anything else which is my responsibility
and in my power to put right.

ving Lord, we gather at your table
e renewed by your life.
n we rise to leave,
us to proclaim the mystery and the wonder
at you have done for us
way we behave
the other sisters and brothers
u love and for whom you died,
d brothers you would have us love,
ke.

He couldn't save himself

> There they crucified him. (John 19.18 REB)
> It was our afflictions he was bearing, our pain he endured ... he was pierced for our transgressions, crushed for our iniquities. (Isaiah 53.4-5 REB)

'He saved others,' they said, 'but he cannot save himself.'
Of course he couldn't;
that was the whole point if only they could have seen it.
At the heart of sin, at the heart of all rebellion against God,
lies self-interest
and saving love had to come
from a completely different mould.
We, who throughout our lives
are driven by self-interest,
see here the one in whom self-interest had no part.

He couldn't save himself
because it wasn't in him to save himself;
all his love and all his power
were directed away from himself to others.
At the cross we are faced with the pain
that lies at the very heart of a loving God.

'Come down from the cross;
if we see that, we shall believe.'
It sounded like a challenge,
but in reality it was the final temptation.
Had Christ been able to come down from the cross
the loving God would have disappeared
and a magician taken his place.

He couldn't save himself:
but from our self-centredness,
from our limited horizons,
from the mean actions
which we clothe with high-sounding principles,
and from all the sins, named and nameless
which fetter us,
and hold us back from the heavenly kingdom,
he can and he will save you and me.

There's a man on a cross

Good Friday. Years A, B & C

> My God, my God, why have you forsaken me? (Psalm 22.1 REB)

There's a man on a cross,
he's there by the roadside;
is it nothing to you
as you pass on your way?

*He is despised and rejected of men; a man of sorrows, and acquainted with grief:
and we hid as it were our faces from him.*

There's a man on a cross,
he hangs by the roadside;
will you look in his eyes
as you pass on your way?

*Surely he hath borne our griefs, and carried our sorrows: yet we did esteem him
stricken, smitten of God, and afflicted.*

There's a man on a cross,
he's nailed by the roadside;
can't you spare him a tear
as you pass on your way?

*He was wounded for our transgressions, he was bruised for our iniquities: the
chastisement of our peace was upon him; and with his stripes we are healed.*

There's a man on a cross,
he's died by the roadside;
won't you mourn for a while,
must you go on your way?

*All we like sheep have gone astray; we have turned every one to his own way; and
the Lord hath laid on him the iniquity of us all.*

There's a man on a cross!

(There's a man on a cross from *Upside Down And Inside Out*
Scripture passages from *Isaiah 53 AV*)

A time of desolation

Holy Saturday. Years A, B & C

> If a man dies, can he live again? (Job 14.12 REB)
> And there, since it was the eve of the Jewish sabbath and the tomb was near at hand, they laid Jesus. (John 19.42 REB)

FIRST DISCIPLE	Last night, just last night we were here together in this room.
SECOND DISCIPLE	'This is my body,' he said, 'broken for you. This is my blood, the blood of the covenant, shed for many.'
FIRST DISCIPLE	But not like this. For God's sake, not like this: us scared out of our wits and him crucified, dead and buried.
SECOND DISCIPLE	Oh, he knew; he knew right enough. He tried hard to prepare us, when you think about it. But what he meant when he took the bread last night and the wine — and what he thought the end would be, we'll never know now. It's finished.
FIRST DISCIPLE	It's finished right enough and the sooner we can leave for Galilee the better.
SECOND DISCIPLE	We've a long wait before it will be safe to do that.

While the disciples are lost in their private world of sorrow, VOICES are heard...

FIRST VOICE	It was a long night and a dark night. A time of fitful sleep and tired hours when sleep refused to come.
SECOND VOICE	A long night and a dark night, and cold and grey the dawn that followed.
THIRD VOICE	Maybe the sun shone and the birds sang, but not for those huddled together in the Upper Room.
FOURTH VOICE	A grey night followed by a grey day, and another night to come before a new week would begin.
FIRST VOICE	Only then would they dare to join the crowds thronging the city streets.
SECOND VOICE	Long silent hours, but elsewhere in the city men could talk as though nothing had happened.

Two PLAYERS now appear in a spotlight

FIRST PLAYER	They say Barabbas has taken to the hills.
SECOND PLAYER	No doubt about it. That's where he was before he was arrested. I give him three months at most.

71

A time of desolation

FIRST PLAYER	But he was pardoned. Freed!
SECOND PLAYER	Can the leopard change his spots? He'll soon be at it again, knifing Romans in the dark, and he'll be caught. There'll be no second Jesus to take his place.
FIRST PLAYER	The man from Nazareth? A good man they say.
SECOND PLAYER	Not good enough to avoid the cross.
FIRST PLAYER	I heard him speak. Twice I heard him. What he said was very disturbing
SECOND PLAYER	Well, he isn't going to disturb anybody else. He's gone on a long journey with a one-way ticket.
	The spotlight fades and the VOICES are heard again
FIRST VOICE	This is the time which is no time and yet is all time.
SECOND VOICE	The hours merge into one another and it matters not whether it is Evening orMidnight.
THIRD VOICE	Midnight or Cockcrow.
FOURTH VOICE	Cockcrow or Morning.
FIRST VOICE	Morning or Afternoon.
SECOND VOICE	Afternoon or Evening.
THIRD VOICE	Evening or Midnight.
	There is a short pause and a change of mood
FOURTH VOICE	The Sabbath is over, a new day has begun.
FIRST VOICE	A new week has begun.
SECOND VOICE	A new era has begun.
THIRD VOICE	For Christ is risen from the dead.
FIRST VOICE	But in the Upper Room it is still the time which is no time.
THIRD VOICE	The men in the Upper Room, unlike Judas, are alive.
FOURTH VOICE	But as yet they are not living.
	The voice of a WATCHMAN is heard as he passes by
WATCHMAN	An hour before the dawn, and all's well. In the Upper Room it is far from well. The darkest of all Sabbaths is past. But as yet there is no glimmer of dawn.

(From *Out Of This World*)

**We pray for any who feel
they have nothing to hope for,
nothing to live for;
any who feel enveloped in stifling darkness.
As the desolation of the disciples
was dispelled by their meeting with the risen Lord,
so may those for whom we pray
be able to hear the message of resurrection
and make it their own.**

Slowly, the dawning

> They put him to death ... but God raised him. (Acts 10.39-40 REB)
> I have seen the Lord! (John 20.18 REB)

It seemed they had come to the end of the way
with nothing to do, but wait the day,
with doorway barred and voices low,
the day when it might be safe to go
away from the city, with all its pain,
away from the memories of death and shame.

Huddled away in an upper room,
with nothing to lift the encircling gloom
darkness around them and darkness within,
a journey to make, but no will to begin,
a group so dejected and so forlorn,
hardly perceiving another dawn.

It wasn't the rays of the morning sun
that led them to know a new age had begun;
that couldn't shatter their sense of loss
who had seen their master nailed to a cross;
but before they were bathed in its evening light
their steps were firm and their eyes were bright:

Something tremendous had happened!
(From *Upside Down And Inside Out*)

Heavenly Father,
if ever you discover us utterly cast down
and giving way to despair,
take hold of us, we pray,
and remind us again that the Easter experience
is for every age and for every person;
that we may know
Christ risen for us, and in us,
holding us in life now and for ever.

Not reform, but revolution!

Easter Sunday. Years A, B & C

> See, I am creating new heavens and a new earth! The past will no more be remembered. (Isaiah 65.17 REB)
> The stone which the builders rejected has become the main corner-stone. (Psalm 118.22 REB)
> He is going ahead of you into Galilee. (Mark 16.7 REB)

Resurrection left the disciples gasping.
Old ways of thinking were destroyed,
old prohibitions swept aside.
They found themselves swept along
into an ocean of new and exciting experiences;
but they wouldn't have been human
if they hadn't occasionally looked back, a little wistfully,
to the golden days when it all began.

Resurrection threatens much that we hold dear.
Not just for Caiaphas, Pilate, or the money-changers;
nearer home, all too many hear the whisper,
'He is risen!' but, fearing change,
strengthen their defences.
Tremendous effort is expended
in propping up the institutional Church;
few dare to ask how effectively it serves
Christ's mission to the world in which we actually live.

What we celebrate at Easter is not the rhythms of nature,
new life springing up after winter sleep.
We are celebrating upheaval and unpredictability;
God acting in such a way
that no one knows what may happen next.
We are celebrating not reform but revolution
and it isn't finished yet!

Risen Lord, may we feel the thrill and the excitement
of your triumph over all that belongs to decay and death.
Help us to overcome all that would hold us back
from playing our part in your revolution.
Enable us to share in your resurrection,
not just some time in the future,
but as a present experience, this very day.

New hope, new life

> You will show me the path of life. (Psalm 16.11 REB)
> He gave us new birth into a living hope. (1 Peter 1.3 REB)
> My Lord and my God. (John 20.28 REB)

When all is dark,
when dreams have failed
and we continually recall times
we would rather forget:
when we despise ourselves
and the devil whispers his lie
that we are worthless;
then, Lord, it is you who gives us
new birth into a living hope.

You tell us
that whatever mess we have made of things
you accept us as we are;
more than that, much more,
you offer us new birth — new life!
You give us fresh grounds for hope
through the knowledge
that we are loved and held secure,
and you help us to discover the confidence
to go out and in turn give hope to others.
You bring to us new birth,
new life,
resurrection!

Lord, through the loving giving of yourself
which makes this personal resurrection possible,
may we grasp the hope,
experience the life,
and share the love,
that we may indeed be part of your new creation.

To those who will receive him, he comes

Second Sunday of Easter. Year B

> The Word of life — this is our theme. (1 John 1.1 NJB)
> Peace be with you! As the Father sent me, so I send you. (John 20.21 REB)

They were frightened,
huddled behind locked doors,
not knowing what to believe;
suddenly he was with them
and they felt the blessing of his peace.

Still he comes
to those who will receive him.
He comes as one who knows
our inmost needs,
our deepest fears,
our most secret sins.
He comes as the great healer,
the loving Saviour,
to make us whole people
and to lead us out from our petty little worlds
into new adventures.

He comes as one who has fought with evil and prevailed;
who has suffered without being destroyed;
who has died and risen again.
He comes,
telling us to have no fear
for the present or the future;
for, whatever lies ahead,
he will be in it with us,
always.

With all my heart, Lord, I would be an Easter person,
sharing in your victory over sin and death.
Help me to look to you for aid in my daily battles,
and lead me in the way you would have me go.

Business as usual?

Second Sunday of Easter. Year C

> 'I am the Alpha and the Omega,' says the Lord God, who is, who was, and who
> is to come, the sovereign Lord of all. (Revelation 1.8 REB)
> We must obey God rather than men. The God of our fathers raised up Jesus ...
> and we are witnesses to all this. (Acts 5.29,30,32 REB)

It was a nasty scare while it lasted;
but things were settling down —
it would soon be 'business as usual'.
Many had been deeply shaken
by that first whisper,
'He is risen',
but as the day progressed
without any further calamities,
they quickly resumed their normal round of activities.

Pilate had washed his hands of the matter saying,
'I must do what is politic and death ends all.'
But what if death doesn't end all?
What if a crucified man should return from the dead?

The religious authorities had defended
the proper procedures of the Church
in the only way they knew.
But what would happen if God
wasn't concerned about the proper procedures,
if you had a situation where you could never know
what the Almighty was going to do next?

It was a nasty scare while it lasted,
but things soon settled down again,
for a while...

Christ is risen! May we never lose our awareness
that this is something to be excited about.
Christ is risen! Our one sure hope in a darkened world.
Christ is risen! God forbid we should ever forget
and say, 'business as usual'.
Lord, be risen in us
that we may live our lives each day
as you would have us live them.

In the breaking of the bread

Third Sunday of Easter. Year A

> How can I repay the Lord for all his benefits to me? I shall lift up the cup of salvation and call on the Lord by name. (Psalm 116.12-13 REB)
> [They] told how he had made himself known to them in the breaking of the bread. (Luke 24.35 REB)

They thought they were inviting a stranger
to share their meal,
until they recognized him
'in the breaking of the bread'.

How often the Gospels tell
of the presence of Jesus enriching a meal.
A multitude is fed on a hillside
and wine provided for a village wedding;
he dines with Martha and Mary
or with Zacchaeus and his dubious friends;
there is the almost unbearable intensity of the Last Supper
and the wondering joy
of a breakfast prepared on the seashore.
His enemies called him a glutton and wine bibber
but many found that a meal in which he shared
was a meal never to be forgotten.

**Too often, Lord, we eat casually,
taking our food and drink for granted,
forgetting the joy of the meal
shared with friends;
forgetting the giver
of the bread and water of life.
As you enriched many a meal with your presence
so enrich ours and teach us
how to make every meal into a sacrament.**

Guilty! yet forgiven

> You asked for the reprieve of a murderer, and killed the Prince of life. But God raised him from the dead; of that we are witnesses. (Acts 3.14-15 REB)
> Consider how great is the love which the Father has bestowed on us in calling us his children! (1 John 3.1 REB)

'You asked for the reprieve of a murderer
and killed the Prince of life,' he cried.
But had they?
How many of those now listening to Peter in the Temple courts
would have been in that early morning crowd
which cried for the release of Barabbas
and the crucifixion of Jesus?
Hardly any —
maybe none —
yet they accepted a collective guilt,
an awareness that they were members of a community
in which such things were part of the way of life.

Lord, we too are guilty,
we too can become intolerant, vindictive;
and quickly react against anything
which appears to threaten our way of life;
or we can let the sorrows of the world
wash over us, saying
that there is nothing we can do about them.
Yet you still love us,
still deal with us,
still take the weight of our sins upon yourself.
Lord, strengthen our will to fight evil,
both within and without,
that we may become a little more worthy
to be called the Father's children.

I will lay me down in peace, and take my rest:
for it is thou, Lord, only,
that makest me dwell in safety. (Psalm 4.9 Book of Common Prayer)

Mary was the first

> Lord my God, I cried to you and you healed me. (Psalm 30.2 REB)
> Worthy is the Lamb who was slain, to receive power and wealth, wisdom and might, honour and glory and praise! (Revelation 5.12 REB)
> Some time later, Jesus showed himself to his disciples once again, by the sea of Tiberias. (John 21.1 REB)

Mary was the first
and she rushed to tell the others,
'Idle tales,' they said, 'idle tales.
Women get emotional,
imagine the impossible.
Idle tales,' they said, 'idle tales.'

Walking to Emmaus,
sharing sorrow with another,
'Have you heard?' they said, 'Have you heard?'
Suddenly they knew him,
rushed back to Jerusalem,
'Have you heard?' they cried, 'Have you heard?'

Fast behind locked doors
and then suddenly he's with them,
'He's alive!' they cried, 'He's alive!'
Speaking words of peace,
reaching out in blessing,
'He's alive!' they cried, 'He's alive!'

Fishing once again
out the whole night catching nothing,
on the shore, he stood, on the shore.
'Cast your nets again,
then come and share my breakfast.'
'It's the Lord!' they cried, 'It's the Lord!'

Joy was mixed with pain
and the pain was self-inflicted,
'We have failed you, Lord, we have failed,
all alone you suffered,
frightened we forsook you,
we have failed you, Lord, we have failed.'
(From *Upside Down And Inside Out*)

Shout it in the street

By his wounds you have been healed. (1 Peter 2.24 REB)
I have come that they may have life, and may have it in all its fullness.
(John 10.10 REB)

Shout it in the street,
tell it to your friend,
spread it through the earth
from end to end;
go to every people,
tell them all to come,
for the Spirit of God
shall make us one.

Listen in the world,
listen in your room,
listen for his call
come late or soon;
ready for adventure,
following his will,
for the Spirit of God
shall lead us still.

Sing aloud for fun,
clap your hands with glee,
dance around with joy
where all can see;
open up your wallet,
find what you can give,
for the Spirit of God
shall make us live.

Everywhere you travel
let everybody see
that the Spirit of God
has set us free.
(From *The Super Skyscraper*)

Lord, live in us and through us,
that we may reflect your glory
today, and every day of our lives.

No other salvation

Fourth Sunday of Easter. Year B

> There is no salvation through anyone else; in all the world no other name has been granted to mankind by which we can be saved. (Acts 4.12 REB)
> Those who keep his commands dwell in him and he dwells in them. (1 John 3.24 REB)
> But there are other sheep of mine, not belonging to this fold; I must lead them as well, and they too will listen to my voice. There will then be one flock, one shepherd. (John 10.16 REB)

No other means of salvation —
none, except through the activity of a God
who became one with us
through a human life,
experiencing rejection, suffering and death
to reach out to estranged humanity.

No other means of salvation —
none, except through the life of the man for others;
the good shepherd
who lays down his life for his sheep.

No other means of salvation —
none, except through a love so great
that it reaches out to enfold
the whole of humanity
holding nothing back,
that whosoever will may be brought within its embrace.

Lord Jesus Christ,
we acknowledge what you have done for us
and the claim you have upon us,
yet we know that we do not follow you as we should.
Forgive us, we pray,
and help us in the fight with the evil
which is never very far from us.
Free us from all arrogance and pretension
and teach us more of your way of love
that our living may open doors
for many others to enter
and enjoy your salvation.

In the valley of the shadow, I will fear no evil

> Yea, though I walk through the valley of the shadow of death, I will fear no evil.
> (Psalm 23.4 Book of Common Prayer)
> The Lamb who is at the centre of the throne will be their shepherd and will guide
> them to springs of the water of life; and God will wipe every tear from their eyes.
> (Revelation 7.17 REB)
> My own sheep listen to my voice; I know them and they follow me. I give them
> eternal life and they will never perish. (John 10.27,28 REB)

Christ is risen!
And we may believe in a life beyond death
which, though it defies all our attempts to describe it,
is the fulfilment of all the deepest longings of the soul.

Christ is risen!
And no past failures need weigh us down;
he will deal with them and free us from their burden
just as surely as he dealt with the failures of his disciples
that first Easter.

Christ is risen!
And we may dare to live our lives today
with him and for him, come what may.
This is the true life, this and no other.

Risen Lord, let your life so flow in me
that my soul may grow
and cast off the shackles
of greed, fear, jealousy, self-assertion,
and all the other things which hold me back
and prevent me from growing into
that which God intended me to be.
And when the time does come
for me to enter the valley of the shadow
may I do so in the confidence
that you will still be with me
and will remain with me for ever.

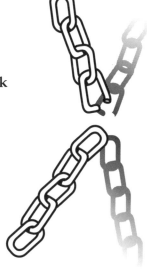

An end — and a beginning

Fifth Sunday of Easter. Year A

> But you are a chosen race ... to proclaim the glorious deeds of him who has called you out of darkness into his marvellous light. (1 Peter 2.9 REB)
> Whoever has faith in me will do what I am doing; indeed he will do greater things still because I am going to the Father. (John 14.12 REB)
> 'Look!' he said, 'I see the heavens opened and the Son of Man standing at the right hand of God.' (Acts 7.56 REB)

Stephen was a Jew
who moved in a wider world
than the Jerusalem authorities.
To the service of the risen Christ
he brought passionate commitment,
impatience with narrow parochialism
and a burning evangelistic zeal;
inevitably he aroused violent opposition.
Charged with blasphemy
he attacked the traditionalists head-on
and was stoned to death by an angry mob.

Stephen's death was a watershed.
It caused others like him to flee Jerusalem
and so, without prior intent, to become missionaries,
spreading their new-found faith far and wide.
But more,
it was the beginning of the process
by which Saul of Tarsus,
fanatical opponent of the young Church,
would become Paul the Apostle,
totally committed to Christ
and the greatest missionary of them all.

Living Lord, you have shown us
that defeat can be transformed into victory,
death become the gateway to life
and the end of things become the beginning of things.
For these mighty wonders, praise be to God.

Set-back — or opportunity?

> Then the angel of the Lord said to Philip, 'Start out and go south to the road that leads down from Jerusalem to Gaza.' (Acts 8.26 REB)
> The coming generation will be told of the Lord; they will make known his righteous deeds. (Psalm 22.30-31 REB)
> This is what love really is: not that we have loved God, but that he loved us. (1 John 4.10 REB)

Forced to leave Jerusalem
following the death of Stephen,
Philip had an overwhelming sense
of being led by the Spirit
into new adventures for Christ.

Many responded to his preaching in normally hostile Samaria
but even as a fellowship of believers was being established
he felt the Spirit urging him on yet again.
Was it chance
that brought him to the carriage
of the Ethiopian Court Official?
If so he grasped that chance
and used it to the full;
the right person in the right place at the right time.
He preached Christ
to a man ready to hear
and who sought immediate baptism.

Now there were two missionaries:
the Officer returning to the Ethiopian Court
and Philip, on his way again,
for his work at this time was to be a planter;
the harvest he must leave to others.

**Lord, when our plans are frustrated,
let us not waste energy bemoaning the fact,
but rather help us to take hold of events
and find ways of using them in your service
and to your glory.**

No more separation

Fifth Sunday of Easter. Year C

Now God has his dwelling with mankind! He will dwell among them and they shall be his people. (Revelation 21.3 REB)
I give you a new commandment: love one another; as I have loved you, so you are to love one another. (John 13.34 REB)

Exiled on Patmos,
John had a vision of a new heaven, a new earth
and a time when there would be no more sea.
To him the sea was a highway for his enemies
and a barrier to his friends,
but he had faith that he was held
in the love of the risen Christ
who overcomes all barriers,
bridges all gulfs.

All separation is painful.
There is an awful finality in death;
no chance to put right a silly misunderstanding,
no chance to share another joke.
But there are other painful forms of separation:
the prisoner locked away,
the loved one far distant,
and the self-inflicted isolation which arises
from our own follies, our sins.

But Christ died to save us all into fullness of life;
he loves us and bids us love one another
so that none, however hard their way,
need ever again feel alone.

And through his saving power,
none whom we have loved and lost
is lost to us for ever.
And sin has no dominion!

Glory to God in the highest!
Christ is risen!
Love has triumphed!
There is no final separation.

Making the unknown known

> To an unknown God. (Acts 17.23 REB)
> Come, listen, all who fear God, and I shall tell you what he has done for me.
> (Psalm 66.16 REB)
> You will know that I am in my Father, and you in me and I in you.
> (John 14.20 REB)

There were gods for every occasion;
gods for war, for love, for travel,
gods of storm and gods of sunshine;
gods for planting, gods for reaping —
you need never be short of an appropriate god.

There was, it must be said, just one problem.
However carefully you might
offer fitting sacrifice
for the aid you were seeking,
you could quite unwittingly overlook
the very god or goddess
whose preserve it was —
and they were so touchy!

So Paul, in Athens, came upon the altar,
dedicated 'To An Unknown God',
where you could offer sacrifice
to the one you might so easily
and unintentionally offend.

And Paul proclaimed that the unknown god
need be unknown no longer.
There was but one God,
infinite, eternal,
yet caring and loving,
all of a piece,
and utterly dependable.

God of all that is and all that is to be,
you have made yourself known to us
through Jesus Christ our Lord;
you alone are God, you alone hold us in life,
you alone reach out to us in immeasurable love;
blessed be your name for ever.

87

Too small a world?

Sixth Sunday of Easter. Year B

> [They] were amazed that the gift of the Holy Spirit should have been poured out even on Gentiles. (Acts 10.45 REB)
> When we love God and obey his commands we love his children too. (1 John 5.2 REB)

Mine is a very little world,
my family, my home and my friends;
it's the dusting and the polishing
the washing and the drying
and the round that never ends.
Not much space for the winds to blow,
not much space for my life to grow,
it's a very little world, I know.

Mine is a very little world,
I hardly ever notice the news;
it's the ironing and the mending,
the shopping and the cooking,
and the wasting time in queues.
Not much space for the winds to blow
not much space for my life to grow,
it's a very little world, I know.

Mine is a very little world,
so fragile, at times I get afraid
and so I'm always busy
and nagging at the children
to slog and make the grade.
Not much space for the winds to blow,
not much space, but where else to go?
It's the only world I know.
(From *One Friday*)

**You amazed the Apostles, Lord,
by giving the Holy Spirit to people
they'd never considered could be part of your family.
Do we also have too small a vision,
live in too confined a space?
We pray that the Holy Spirit may widen our horizons
and make us ready to venture into uncharted territories.**

Strange contradictions

Cross over to Macedonia and help us. (Acts 16.9 REB)
The leaves of the trees are for the healing of the nations. (Revelation 22.2 REB)
Peace is my parting gift to you, my own peace, such as the world cannot give.
Set your troubled hearts at rest, and banish your fears. (John 14.27 REB)

The Upper Room
His disciples are anxious, uncertain, fearful;
soon they will flee
and Jesus will take his lonely road to the cross.
'Peace is my gift to you,' he says;
peace, not as freedom from trouble — but in the midst of trouble:
peace, not as freedom from pain — but in the midst of pain:
the peace of God — which passes human understanding.

Troas
It was to have been a missionary journey
but they met with obstacle after obstacle,
frustration after frustration;
to Paul this meant God must have other plans,
but what could they be?
And then the dream —
'Cross over to Macedonia' —
and the gospel entered Europe.

Patmos
One of an unpopular, persecuted minority,
John dreams, not in terms of revenge,
but of a new order
of a heavenly city with, at its heart,
a broad avenue of trees
whose leaves are 'for the healing of the nations'.

Almighty God,
help me to trust you to bring good
out of the most unpromising situations;
help me to pray and work
for 'the healing of the nations';
and in the stormiest days
enable me to know myself
enfolded in your peace.

Caught up into the Godhead

Ascension of the Lord. Years A, B, C

And in the act of blessing he parted from them. (Luke 24.51 REB)
He put all things in subjection beneath his feet, and gave him as head over all
things to the church which is his body. (Ephesians 1.22 REB)

'In the act of blessing he parted from them.'
A blessing:
the last word of the old age,
the first word of the new;
setting the seal on what lay behind,
holding promise for what lies ahead.

In Jesus,
all the ups and down of human experience,
all its hopes and fears,
joys and sorrows,
are caught up into the Godhead.
The knowledge of what it is to be human
is part of the very nature of God.

But also,
freed from the limitations of time and space,
in every age,
wherever they may be,
Jesus will be with his people.

We would be your people, Lord,
though, like the Apostles,
we have little idea of what may lie ahead of us,
what must be left behind as we travel,
what new frontiers wait to be crossed.
But we believe
that you will be with us in our journeying,
meeting us with blessing;
and in that confidence
we can face the future
with hope and with expectancy.

A matter of knowing our limitations

> It is not for you to know about dates or times. (Acts 1.7 REB)
> He cares for you, so cast all your anxiety on him. (1 Peter 5.7 REB)
> ...that they may be one, as we are one. (John 17.11 REB)

Not for us to know times or seasons,
not even for us to be dogmatic
about the Church's calendar,
ritual,
or government.
Only by acknowledging
that we do not know,
do not possess
a whole or exclusive truth;
only by casting ourselves on him
who cares for all of us
can we begin to discover the means
by which we may eventually become one.

Living God,
help us to take to heart
your word of unity
spoken to us in our Lord Jesus Christ.
Show us how to break down
the barriers which still divide
your people from one another.
Shake us out of our acceptance of division
and, as we offer thanksgiving
for the saints in heaven,
save us from imagining them
all to be our sort of people.
Teach us to revel
in the diversity of the Church
which, welcomed and embraced,
can only enrich our experience
and heighten the joy
of being called to be citizens
in your kingdom.

Living in the real world

Seventh Sunday of Easter. Year B

> They drew lots, and the lot fell to Matthias. (Acts 1.26 REB)
> I do not pray you to take them out of the world, but to keep them from the evil one. (John 17.15 REB)

That's our job!

To live in the world,
the world as it is,
the real world;
the world where issues are seldom clear-cut
and procedures are imperfect,
even for the choosing of a new Apostle.

And we have to make choices,
and we can get it wrong;
even when we are convinced that we are right
— *especially when we are convinced that we are right!*
And we have to go on living in the world,
the world as it is,
the real world,
the world where we can't hope
to keep ourselves spotless
however much we try.

That's our job!

Lord, give us the wisdom
and the humility
to recognize that not everything
that seems right to us,
however passionately we may believe it,
will necessarily be in accordance with
the will of the Holy Spirit.
In a world where the division between
good and evil is seldom clear-cut,
help us to choose as wisely as we can,
but save us from being arrogant about our opinions.
Teach us to listen to others
and never allow us to forget
that we may sometimes be wrong.

That we might be one

> I am the Alpha and the Omega, the first and the last, the beginning and the end. (Revelation 22.13 REB)
> With me in them and you in me, may they be so perfected in unity that the world will recognize that it was you who sent me. (John 17.23 NJB)

That we may be one in purpose
Father, we thank you for the many people
of different nations, colour, languages and traditions
who have heard and responded
to the call to be
part of the people of God,
part of the body of Christ.
We thank you that together with them
we are privileged to belong
to a world-wide church.
We confess that we are far from being
one in purpose, spirit and love,
as our Lord prayed we should be;
and we ask your help
that we may
better understand one another,
willingly learn from one another,
and together grow closer to you.

That all our gifts may be used
Bountiful God,
we often fail to use as fully as we should
the gifts you have given to us,
and sometimes we totally fail
to recognize the gifts you have given to others.
We ask that you will enlarge our understanding
and increase our willingness
to pool and use all your gifts,
that the life and witness of our churches
may be enriched
and bring added blessings
both to those within
and to those beyond our fellowships.

Pentecostal prayers

Day of Pentecost. Years A, B & C

> They were all amazed and perplexed, saying to one another,
> 'What can this mean?' (Acts 2.12 REB)
> I wish that all the Lord's people were prophets and that the Lord would bestow his spirit on them all! (Numbers 11.29 REB)
> Can these bones live? (Ezekiel 37.3 REB)
> Set your troubled hearts at rest, and banish your fears. (John 14.27 REB)

Come, Holy Spirit, come!
Gloriously unfettered Spirit,
working amongst us in ways beyond our conceiving,
breaking down our carefully defined boundaries,
renewing life where all seemed beyond hope:
Spirit of exuberant power,
Spirit of calm and peace,
touch our lives where and how you will,
shake us if you must, but come!

Love
Spirit of Love,
who seeks that which may be loved
in each and every one of us,
help us in our turn
to recognize lovingly
the true worth and the real needs
of our family and our friends,
and to behave caringly
towards all whom we shall meet this day.

Joy
Spirit of Joy,
dwell in us, we pray,
and enable us to discover life
in all the fullness which our Lord came to bring.
Save us from pursuing short-lived pleasures
which leave a bitter taste
and be as an ever-renewing spring within our hearts,
so that we may learn to cherish every blessing
and always have reason to rejoice.

Pentecostal prayers

Peace
Spirit of Peace,
you know the things which unnecessarily disturb us
because we have not yet learned
how to put ourselves fully into the hands of God;
stay with us, we pray,
that the little space we have made for you
may grow until we are fully possessed
of that peace which passes human understanding.

Patience
Patient Spirit,
deal with our restlessness
and lead us into the ways of tranquillity;
but save us from confusing patience
with indolence or indifference.
Teach us the art of waiting
when waiting is required,
but help us to wait as those who are ready for action
when the moment for action arises.

Kindness
Holy Spirit,
your kindness never smothers us
or makes us feel uncomfortably beholden.
Help us to learn from you:
show us how to be compassionate
without laying down conditions;
how to practise kindness without attaching strings
and how to give without expecting return.
Holy Spirit, let your strong kindness
flow in us and shape our ways.

Goodness
Holy Spirit,
forgive us if we still find it hard to believe
that goodness is not a matter of keeping ourselves clean,
but rather of being ready to become besmirched
in the effort to give help where help is needed.
Remind us, when we need reminding,
that we are called
not so much to be good as to do good;
not so much to follow a code
as to walk in the way of our Lord.

Pentecostal prayers

Fidelity
Holy Spirit,
your faithfulness is beyond all our deserving,
for, however often we fail,
you do not write us off
but continue to deal with us in love.
Strengthen, guide and help us, we pray,
that we may reflect something of your fidelity
in our own daily living.

Gentleness
Gentle Spirit,
you never abuse your awesome power,
but rather seek to mend that which is broken
and to make strong that which is weak;
build up in us the strength we shall need
if we are to be truly gentle;
that we may treat all men and women,
whatever their condition,
with that respect and care
with which you have ever dealt with us.

Self-control
Holy Spirit,
part of the undivided Godhead,
teach us, torn so many ways
by conflicting desires and emotions
to be 'all of a piece'.
Help us to gain the victory
over unruly longings and passions
and bring us to that self-control
which is revealed
not in a 'buttoned up' personality
but in one which can be
venturesome and outgoing
because it has found its security in you.

Song of the heavens

> And God saw all that he had made, and it was very good. (Genesis 1.31 REB)
> Lord our sovereign, how glorious is your name throughout the world!
> (Psalm 8.1 REB)

At the birth of all that has ever been created
sound flooded out in rippling waves,
sound before ever there were ears for hearing,
sound to proclaim to the Lord of days.

> Praise to the thought that dreamed us,
> praise to the skill that made us,
> praise to the God who orders all
> and evermore sustains us.

And the stars sang out to the glory of their Maker,
sang as they moved at a gathering pace,
sang as they twinkled in the new-made heavens,
sang as they danced through the clear, clean space.

> Praise to the thought that dreamed us,
> praise to the skill that made us,
> praise to the God who orders all
> and evermore sustains us.

And the music swelled to the glory of the Maker,
swelled in a pattern of a million chords,
swelled as it echoed through the whole creation,
swelled to the glory of the Lord of Lords.

> Praise to the thought that dreamed us,
> praise to the skill that made us,
> praise to the God who orders all
> and evermore sustains us.

(From *The Maker Of Things*)

An all-embracing love

> The whole earth is full of his glory. (Isaiah 6.3 REB)
> Ascribe to the Lord glory and might. (Psalm 29.1 REB)
> God so loved the world... (John 3.16 REB)

Holy and glorious God,
you are far beyond the reach of our finite minds,
yet through the Holy Spirit
you have made yourself known to us
by many witnesses,
and, above all,
you meet us
in the life, death and resurrection
of our Lord Jesus Christ.

Through him we know you as a God of love;
a love which enfolds the whole of creation:
and we believe
you call us to respond to that love,
to be numbered amongst those
who,
knowing themselves loved,
have the confidence
to seek to share that love.

Like Isaiah of old,
we know that we ourselves
are part of the human problem;
yet we dare to pray,
take us, poor instruments that we are,
and let your love grow within us
until it overflows
into the lives of others,
that they too may come to know
that you love them
and that you will hold them fast
now and for ever.

The Spirit of Truth

Hear how wisdom calls ... The Lord created me the first of his works.
(Proverbs 8.1,22 REB)
Through the Holy Spirit he has given us, God's love has flooded our hearts.
(Romans 5.5 REB)
The Spirit of Truth ... will guide you into all the truth. (John 16.13 REB)

'My dear, dear children,
use all your skills and experience;
use to the full
all the talents I have given you;
but do ask yourselves from time to time
where you are going
and what it is that awaits you at the end of your journey.

'Take for your guide the Spirit of Truth,
not **'the truth '**, discerned with blinkered vision
which leads to indifference to the perceptions of others,
intolerance of dissenting opinions,
arrogant and overbearing self-righteousness,
fanaticism, crusades and persecutions.

'Not **'the truth'** which is really a terrible falsehood,
but the 'Spirit of Truth',
which bears witness to Jesus Christ.
This is the truth which will set you free;
free from the need to assert yourselves,
free from the need to promote yourselves,
free to listen, to share, to learn and to love.

'Let the Spirit lead you into the Truth
which is so much greater
than all your little truths,
into Love
much greater
than anything you have so far experienced,
and into Life
which nothing can take from you.

'Give yourself into the hands of the Spirit of Truth —
and be re-created, be reborn.'

Silhouettes

(4) May 29 - June 4. Year A

> Make yourself an ark. (Genesis 6.14 REB)
> The rain came down, the floods rose, the winds blew. (Matthew 7.25 REB)
> So we are not afraid though the earth shakes. (Psalm 46.2 REB)
> I am not ashamed of the gospel. It is the saving power of God. (Romans 1.16 REB)

A frail craft,
carried by wind and current
on a mighty flood,
yet riding the storm.

A house,
battered by tempest,
but, built on rock,
standing
while much else is swept away.

A God, utterly dependable,
who in the face of ecological disasters,
social disintegration,
and death itself,
provides enduring refuge.

**God of all our days,
we cannot know where
or when in our lives
the tempest may strike,
but we believe you are a God
who reaches out to hold us fast
and especially in the time of trouble.
Strengthen our faith and our trust, we pray,
and draw us ever closer to yourself,
that we may know ourselves
held secure in your loving care,
this day and for ever.**

God's ways are not our ways

> Yet we who have this spiritual treasure are like common clay pots.
> (2 Corinthians 4.7 GNB)

That's us, common clay pots.
If he'd been alive today
Paul might have written
'cheap plastic boxes'.
The wonder is that our God
is willing to risk his treasure
in such poor containers.

Make me aware, my God,
of the work you have for me to do
despite all my weaknesses,
and strengthen my will to do it
to the very best of my ability.

How mysterious, God, are your thoughts to me. (Psalm 139.17 REB)
The sabbath was made for man, not man for the sabbath. (Mark 2.27 REB)

Not so very long ago,
Sundays could be depressing
with so many of the things we wanted to do
deemed inappropriate for the Lord's Day.
Today anything goes,
we can do what we like.
Shopping malls are open,
car boot sales abound,
motorways are jammed with traffic.
Yet many still find Sunday depressing,
Sunday,
the day given for our re-creation,
Sunday,
a time for joy and for refreshing.

Lord, where did we lose our way?

A lonely witness

> He repaired the altar of the Lord ... the fire of the Lord fell, consuming
> the whole offering... (1 Kings 18.30,38 REB)

Physically exhausted
and silent at last,
the priests of Baal
watched with hostile eyes
as Elijah,
needing all his strength
to lift the stones into place,
repaired the altar of the Lord.
They watched
and they waited.
When the king gave the sign
they would pounce
and destroy him.

At last the altar was rebuilt.
Elijah prepared the sacrifice
and offered the evening prayer.
The whole silent, waiting crowd
found the tension almost unbearable.
Suddenly,
the fire of the Lord fell!
Elijah was vindicated!

But there are times
when the Lord does not answer by fire.

**Lord, help me, I pray,
and teach me ever more of your ways
that both when your power is seen
and when it is hidden,
I may with integrity
witness to the truths I have received,
to the truths by which I live.**

No easy thing, being chosen

> Abram journeyed by stages. (Genesis 12.9 REB)
> Abraham had faith — when hope seemed hopeless.
> (Romans 4.17,18 REB)

He didn't always get it right of course,
who does?
But, having heard the call,
his purpose was to travel,
with God,
as best he could,
until he reached his journey's end,
whatever that end might be.
Time and again
he had to build a fresh altar.
Never could he say,
'Now I need go no further.'
All his life he was a traveller.
All his life he remained a pilgrim.

And so the 'Father of many nations'
bequeathed to his descendants
the gifts
       — of listening for a half-heard voice,
       — of following an unending pilgrim quest,
       — and the faith that the end of the journey
          lies with God.

Travelling God,
strengthen our will to travel with you
wherever you would have us go.
We cannot know
where our journey will lead,
but we pray that we may never
lose our awareness
that you are travelling with us
and that you will be there to receive us
at the end of the way.

The unforgivable sin

(5) June 5 - June 11. Year B

> Truly I tell you: every sin and every slander can be forgiven; but whoever slanders the Holy Spirit can never be forgiven; he is guilty of an eternal sin. (Mark 3.28 REB)

As a young man, John Bunyan went through agonies of soul-searching, as he tells in *Grace Abounding To The Chief Of Sinners*. At one point he writes: 'About this time I took an opportunity to break my mind to an ancient Christian, and told him all my case; I told him, also, that I was afraid that I had sinned the sin against the Holy Ghost; and he told me that he thought so too. Here, therefore, I had but cold comfort; but, talking a little more with him, I found him, though a good man, a stranger to much combat with the devil. Wherefore I went to God again, as well as I could, for mercy still.' (para 180)

In Jesus we see a love which knows no limits and which willingly takes the way of the cross to rescue a fallen world. In the light of such a love, the unforgivable sin has to be something more than the uttering of words, however foul. Surely the only soul for whom there can be no forgiveness is the soul that seeks none; who cannot be forgiven because all forgiveness is utterly rejected. Whether any soul can resist the love of God to all eternity is another matter; but the gospel message is clear: the man or woman who longs and seeks to be embraced by that love which we see in Jesus Christ will not be turned away.

Yes, Lord, I know it, I do grieve the Holy Spirit.
Too many times I blur the edges of good and evil
and turn from light to the less demanding shadows.
Whilst choices are seldom
a simple matter of black or white,
I confess that my way is often
a good deal greyer than it should be.
In your mercy, Lord,
don't let me get away with it;
keep pricking my conscience;
help me to recognize when I am astray
that I may return to you for forgiveness.
Lord, renew my vision and strengthen my will
to resist evil and to do good;
in the greatness of your love,
Lord, hear my prayer.

In time of famine

> The jar of flour did not give out, nor did the flask of oil fail, as the word of the Lord foretold through Elijah. (1 Kings 17.16 REB)

A widow's story
You ask, 'What was he like, the man of God?'
A countryman, who lived simply,
taking hardship in his stride.
The day he came
I was near to death;
the rains had failed again,
the fields were parched
and the barn empty.
My husband not long dead,
I had no family near, except my son,
and he but a child.
There was nothing left
but a handful of flour
and a little oil
and I was gathering fuel enough
to bake us one last loaf
when he appeared.
He asked for food and drink,
and so he came to lodge,
labouring to keep us,
until the drought was ended.
Nor was that all.
One awful day
when I thought my son was dead,
he healed him.
Yes, I gave the man shelter,
but much, much more,
he gave us life.

Lord, should you confront me today
in one of your needy ones,
let me not refuse to listen
to that which you would ask of me,
lest in failing to share,
I fail to receive blessing you would give.

Freely we received

(6) June 12 - June 18. Year A

> How can I repay the Lord? (Psalm 116.12 REB)
> You received without cost; give without charge. (Matthew 10.8 REB)

Day by day
they pass our churches,
some hurrying, some idling;
but how do they see us,
those men and women in the street?
What impression have we left on them?
Do they see anything more than
a weather-worn poster
appealing for money
or telling of events long past?
Do they wonder
what we are doing
on the rare occasions that the doors are open?
Do they ever give a thought
to why those buildings are there?
Should they?
Have we any reason to hope
that some might see us as living communities,
with something really desirable
which they too could share?
Would we want them to do so?

Bountiful God,
we often fail to use
as fully as we should
the gifts you have given to us,
and sometimes we totally fail
to recognize the gifts you have given to others.
Enlarge our understanding
and increase our willingness
to pool and use all your gifts,
that the life and witness
of our churches may be enriched
and bring added blessings
both to those within
and to those beyond our walls.

Whatever next?

For anyone united to Christ, there is a new creation: the old order has gone; a new order has already begun. (2 Corinthians 5.17 REB)

Whatever next? People are so credulous,
never before have I heard such a thing;
that Galilean, you know, the preacher,
now they are saying that he is a king!
If you believe a stupid thing like that
you might as well say
perhaps the world is round — instead of flat.

Whatever next? People will say anything;
now it's a man who's come back from the dead;
you must be joking, they must be barmy,
if you ask me they're just gone in the head.
If you can swallow such a crazy tale
you might as well say
that a man could cross the seas — without a sail.

Whatever next? Have you heard the latest one?
You know that fellow, the man we saw die,
people are saying — can you imagine? —
now he is Lord of the earth and sky.
I'll bet they're going to have to change their tune!
You might as well say
that a man could reach the moon.
You might as well say that Rome will crumble,
say that the Empire's had its day!
Might as well say I could talk to my editor
when he's a thousand miles away.

Whatever next? People are suggestible,
they'll swallow anything however indigestible.
Well, anyway, we are not so gullible,
whatever will it be — next?
('Reporter's Song' from *One Friday* picturing a present-day style press
conference being briefed on the resurrection)

Standing in the way of progress

> You have sold yourself to do what is wrong in the eyes of the Lord.
> (1 Kings 21.20 REB)

It stood in the way of progress,
a solitary vineyard,
Naboth's vineyard;
Naboth, a stubborn peasant who wouldn't give an inch,
wouldn't consider even the most generous offers
and so, in the end...

It had been a matter of improvements to the palace gardens
but it could have been
an industrial development,
a motorway,
an airport,
a dam...

Naboth's property didn't have to be a vineyard;
it might have been a heritage site
or a rain forest;
it might not even have been appropriated at all,
merely ruined
by uncontrolled pollution.

When negotiation failed
Ahab had been easily persuaded
to use other means to obtain what he wanted.
He entered into possession of the vineyard,
but in the end,
there was a price
he hadn't reckoned on
to be paid.

Teach us, Lord, to have proper respect
for the rights of others;
especially those who have little,
especially those who in our eyes
are awkward and stubborn.
Teach us, so that when disputes do arise
we are working with you, not against.

Also children of God

> Then God opened her eyes and she saw a well full of water. (Genesis 21.19 REB)
> Listen, Lord ... for I am oppressed and poor ... your love towards me is great, and you have rescued me. (Psalm 86.1,13 REB)

Had she been born into slavery,
sold by her parents to buy bread,
or captured in some plundering raid?
To Abraham
Hagar was simply property.
She bore him a son,
which was well enough
until Isaac came along;
then her presence became an embarrassment
and a source of conflict.

She had to go.

But where should
a single mother with her child
go in a wilderness?
The provisions Abraham provided
were soon exhausted.
Saved from almost certain death
she learned the great truth
that to God
she and her child
were persons of infinite worth
and they were in the Almighty's care,
just as much as Abraham.

**Lord, help me to learn more of what
it means to love and care for others
and if I am ever tempted
to say that I've had enough of someone,
whatever the reason,
remind me
that you have never yet said that about me.**

Ready for battle?

> Then (David) picked up his stick, chose five smooth stones from the wadi, and put them in a shepherd's bag which served as his pouch and, sling in hand, went to meet the Philistine. (1 Samuel 17.40 REB)
> We wield the weapons of righteousness in right hand and left.
> (2 Corinthians 6.7 REB)

The sling
and the five smooth stones
with which David set out
to meet Goliath
were hardly impressive,
and certainly couldn't be classed
as sophisticated equipment;
but these he had learned to use,
and they were enough.

Does that mean, Lord,
that we also must discover simple,
but appropriate weapons
for the battles we shall face
with our own particular giants?
Such as the weapons of righteousness —
      innocent behaviour,
      patience,
      kindliness,
      unaffected love —
weapons you provide
through the Holy Spirit.

**Lord, let me be quietly alert,
ready for any battles which may await me;
but let me also be at peace with myself
in the confidence that whatever lies ahead
you will be there;
I shall not have to face it on my own.**

Greater than he knew

> There is no such thing as Jew and Greek, slave and freeman, male and female; for you are all one person in Christ Jesus. (Galatians 3.28 REB)

All these divisions are false,'
cried Paul,
declaring through the Holy Spirit,
truths with far greater implications
than he could ever
have possibly imagined.

Two thousand years have passed,
and still we have not grasped
that God is blind
to differences which can tear us apart,
that God is blind:
>>> to colour,
>>> race,
>>> sex
>>> wealth,
>>> and social status.

All are the children of the Almighty,
and his provision is intended
for the whole of humankind.

Save us, Lord,
from either fearing
or seeking to exploit
those who are different from ourselves
and show us the joys which can arise
from our diversity
and the sharing of the variety of the gifts
with which we have been blessed.

The will of God?

(8) June 26 - July 2. Year A

> Take your son ... offer him as a sacrifice. (Genesis 22.2 REB)
> God gives freely, and his gift is eternal life. (Romans 6.23 REB)

What prompted Abraham
to imagine that God
required him to kill his son, Isaac,
and offer him as a sacrifice?
Was it deep-rooted guilt
because he had driven out Hagar
and her child Ishmael?
Was it the fact that he lived among peoples
who regularly sacrificed their children
to placate vengeful deities?
Whatever it was that caused Abraham
to set out with this intention,
his hand was stayed,
and he learned
that this is not what the Lord requires;
that what is asked of us
is the offering
not of death
but of life.

Heavenly Father,
may we never lose the awareness
that when we offer you our lives
you give them back to us
richer than we brought them;
may we never doubt
that your whole nature is love
and it is your delight
not to deprive
but to enrich your children.

Jairus looks back

> For in the Lord is love unfailing, and great is his power to deliver.
> (Psalm 130.7 REB)
> 'My little daughter is at death's door,' he said. 'I beg you to come and lay your hands on her.' (Mark 5.23 REB)

Jairus
See, our first grandchild,
our daughter's son...

Thank you, yes,
his mother's well —
more, she is radiant.
The child brings us a double joy
because there was a time
we thought we'd never see this day,
thought she was dead.
Ah, you've heard the story?...

Yes,
blessed be God,
Jesus of Nazareth
restored her to us...

No, my friend,
he is not dead.
True, he was crucified...

Oh I freely acknowledge
we have become
followers of The Way,
but who,
given the choice,
would not follow a path
which leads
from death to life?

Lord, we praise you for the knowledge
that, even when the time comes
that bodily sickness cannot be healed,
you will still be holding us in life
which nothing can destroy.

I've said it before

> You were called to be free; do not use your freedom as an opening for self-indulgence. (Galatians 5.13 NJB)

I've said it before
and I'll say it again,
I'm going to be firm
well, I think that I am.
Tomorrow I'll start,
I shall have to be tough,
but I think that I know
when enough is enough.

So I'll cut out the cakes
and the fats and the cream,
the ices and sweets
till they're only a dream.
I'm going to be firm,
tomorrow is the day I start —
but tonight — tonight...

So I'll cut out the tales,
the tittle and tattle,
the scandalous stories,
the gossip and prattle,
my lips shall be sealed,
tomorrow is the day I start —
but tonight — tonight...

So I'll cut out the rows,
not another harsh word;
my nagging is done,
not a sound shall be heard.
I'm all sweetness and light,
tomorrow is the day I start —
but tonight — tonight...
The devil may have tonight!
(From *One Friday*)

On the other hand the fruit of the Spirit is love, joy, peace, patience, kindness, goodness, trustfulness, gentleness and self-control. (Galatians 5.22 NJB)

Help when help is needed

The good which I want to do, I fail to do; but what I do is the wrong which is against my will. (Romans 7.19 REB)
How can I describe this generation? They are like children sitting in the market-place and calling to each other, We piped for you and you would not dance. We lamented, and you would not mourn. (Matthew 11.16,17 REB)
Come to me, all who are weary and whose load is heavy; I will give you rest. (Matthew 11.28 REB)

Patient and loving Lord,
how precious are your words of invitation,
'Come to me, all who are weary
and whose load is heavy.'
And how precious is the knowledge
that however many times we fail to do
even the good we recognize,
you do not abandon us,
but are still present to help.

Lord, we don't need to tell you
that behind all outward appearances
of self-assurance
we are often uncertain and insecure
and only too conscious
that we have made a mess of things.
Even when we pray
we don't know our true needs.
With deep thankfulness
we hold on to the knowledge
that when all other words fail
we may say,
'Into your hands,
we commit ourselves...'
and trust that the prayer
we have been unable to formulate
will nevertheless be heard.

Strong in weakness

(9) July 3 - July 9. Year B

Where does he get it from? ... Is he not the carpenter? ... So they turned against him ... And he was unable to do any miracle there. (Mark 6.2-5 REB)
My grace is all you need; power is most fully seen in weakness.
(2 Corinthians 12.9 REB)

Even Jesus wasn't successful all the time,
yet it must have hurt him
to be rejected,
and to find himself virtually powerless
in his home village.

Paul came to accept
rejection and ill-treatment
as a badge of honour;
but he still prayed hard
to be freed
from a physical disability
which incapacitated him
in a way that made him a laughing stock
to his enemies.
But there was to be no let-up.
The answer he received to his prayers was,
'Stick it out.
My grace is all you need.'

Lord, we hate being caught off balance,
hate being made to look silly;
so it's hard for us to accept
that there will be times when we are called,
not only to do things which are painful,
but also to act in ways
which make us look foolish.
When those times come,
do remind us again
that we have to forget our dignity
if we are to follow the way
of a crucified Saviour;
and help us in our vulnerability
to commit ourselves afresh to your loving care.

The nature of mission

After this the Lord appointed a further seventy-two and sent them on ahead in pairs to every town and place he himself intended to visit. (Luke 10.1 REB)

'Go,' he said.
'Go as messengers
and prepare the way for me,
that when I come
I may be welcomed.

'Go simply,
carry no surplus baggage,
take with you nothing,
but the good news
of the kingdom of God.

'Go helpfully,
gladly give aid and comfort
whenever you have opportunity.

'Go peacefully,
tell of the kingdom
to those who will receive you,
but when you are rejected,
pass quietly on your way.

'Go joyfully,
for though you may appear
to have little or nothing,
you in fact have
everything of enduring worth.'

**Loving Lord,
blow upon the sparks of love
that are in my heart
and kindle a flame
in which others may recognize you
and be glad.**

Not the most promising material

(10) July 10 - July 16. Year A

> Sell me your rights as the firstborn. (Genesis 25.31 REB)

Not the most attractive of characters.
Jacob was quite ready
to steal from his brother
and trick his father;
yet God used him,
gradually educating him,
gradually leading him
towards more responsible living.

Jacob would never be
a shining angel of light,
but which of us is?
With all his imperfections
God took hold of him
and gave him a place in his purposes,
and if God could do that with Jacob
maybe he could
make something of me.

**I thank you, Lord, for the knowledge
that the men and women
you have used in your service
have not been plaster saints,
but have been people
with passions and moods,
faults as well as virtues,
failures as well as successes.
So I ask you
to take me as I am,
make of me what you will,
but let me be numbered
amongst those who have served you
in spite of all my failings.**

A troubled king

> But when Herod heard of it, he said, 'This is John, whom I beheaded, raised from the dead.' (Mark 6.16 REB)
> In Christ our release is secured and our sins forgiven through the shedding of his blood. (Ephesians 1.7 REB)

A Security Officer reports to Herod Antipas
Not so, my Lord,
it is not the baptizer;
I can assure you
John has not returned from the dead.
No, this is a new man,
and we are watching him closely,
very closely indeed.
He is another named Jesus,
and nothing of consequence,
merely an upstart journeyman from Nazareth.
Some of John's followers
have transferred to him;
wild flights of imagination
call him a prophet,
Elijah, even Messiah;
but he is none of these
and though at this present time
many are flocking to him
there are few of note among them.
The novelty will soon wear off.
He has a silken tongue
but will overreach himself
as they all do,
and then...
he will trouble you no further.

**Lord, may we have the humility,
the respect for others,
the openness to new truths
and the desire to live lovingly,
which will enable us to recognize you
when you come amongst us.**

At an inn in Jericho

(10) July 10 - 16. Year C

> I am setting a plumb-line in the midst of my people Israel. (Amos 7.8 REB)
> But a Samaritan who was going that way came upon him, and when he saw him
> he was moved to pity... (Luke 10.33 REB)

An Innkeeper
You are brother to the injured man?
He is much stronger now
and can travel with you,
but you must go carefully.
Yes, he was on his way down from Jerusalem
when he was set upon and robbed;
as you say, sir, a most dangerous road.
When the merchant found him
he was more dead than alive,
but the merchant
tended him with no little skill
and brought him here.
That was some few weeks back.
You look troubled, sir,
are you thinking of the reckoning?
If that is all
you may forget it;
that same merchant who found him
has paid in full,
giving me the final sum
just before you came.
Yes, sir, he is indeed a noble man,
I have come to know him well
and have great respect for him.
Your brother was aware
as he lay helpless,
that others saw him, but passed by;
a priest, a Levite, maybe more
before the merchant stopped
to give him aid.
You ask me who he is, this merchant?
He was leaving us as you arrived, sir —
that's right,
the man you spat at as he passed,
the Samaritan!

The field is the world

> Examine me, God, and know my mind; test me, and understand my anxious thoughts. Watch lest I follow any path that grieves you; lead me in the everlasting way. (Psalm 139.23,24 REB)
> The Spirit of God affirms to our spirit that we are God's children. (Romans 8.16 REB)
> The field is the world. (Matthew 13.38 REB)

Forgive our insularity
Holy Spirit, one with the Father and the Son,
forgive us when we try to take
little corners of your work
and claim them for our own.
Forgive us when we lose our sense of proportion
and forget that we are called to be
part of a far greater purpose;
when we forget that we are called to be partners
in a great world-wide fellowship of witnesses
to the gospel faith.
Forgive us, and so guide us
that our future conduct may be more worthy
of the gospel of Christ our Lord.

May we recognize your presence
Everlasting God,
Father, Son and Holy Spirit,
when we look on the beauty of the world
may we recognize your beauty;
when we meet generosity,
kindness, goodness
in other men and women,
may we recognize your grace.
Beyond the sins of the world
may we know your salvation,
and in pain and in suffering
may we know you as one
who bears it with us,
that in all things and in all places
we may know you near,
and near to bless.

Not a museum or a theme park

(11) July 17 - July 23. Year B

> I lived in a tent and a tabernacle. (2 Samuel 7.6 REB)
> In him the whole building is bonded together and grows into a holy temple in the
> Lord. (Ephesians 2.21 REB)

Across the centuries
breathtakingly beautiful churches, abbeys and cathedrals
have been built to the glory of God.
We have a wonderful heritage,
but even the noblest buildings wear out
and can only be maintained
at ever-increasing cost.

Not that we should grudge the expense,
but is that really what the Lord requires?
Top priority?
The more magnificent the building
the greater the danger of it becoming
a museum or a theme park,
complete with entrance fee and guided tours,
crowded with sightseers of course —
but what if God
is waiting outside for us,
in the rain?

Paul saw a different dwelling place for God;
one built of human lives,
moving, changing,
constantly being renewed.
A dwelling as mobile
as the tent of the wilderness years,
the 'dream years'
when it seemed that God was ever close at hand.

Whatever church buildings we may have inherited, Lord,
help us to use them wisely and imaginatively
as we seek to witness to your love for all your people.
And fit us, we pray, to be part of the living temple
'founded on the apostles and the prophets
with Christ Jesus himself as the corner-stone'.

A woman's place

> To present each one of you as a mature member of Christ's body.
> (Colossians 1.28 REB)
> Mary has chosen what is best; it shall not be taken away from her.
> (Luke 10.42 REB)

Martha
'So this is Martha,' you say to yourself,
'the housewife who got into a right state
over entertaining a few guests
and lost patience with her sister
when she failed to give a hand.'
No, no excuses,
you may feel sympathy for me,
many do,
but the image remains;
a woman who couldn't see beyond
her immediate domestic concerns.

I was busy that day, of course I was,
but I was used to managing
and had help enough.
No, I was concerned for Mary;
I loved her dearly
but she had no sense of what is proper.
Don't you understand?
She shouldn't have been sitting there with the men,
it could easily set tongues awagging.
A man's world is different, starting from synagogue;
we have our separate places, our separate functions;
she was where she had no right to be —
or so I thought.
Well, the Lord saw it differently,
and who am I to quarrel with him?
But I do sometimes wonder where it will all end.

Thank you, Lord, for accepting us all, just as we are,
men, women; young, old; wealthy, poor...
Thank you that the distinctions we draw
have no meaning for you,
that your gifts are for all and your call is to all.

A kingdom of many surprises

(12) July 24 - July 30. Year A

> The kingdom of Heaven is like... (Matthew 13.31 REB)
> Nothing in all creation ... can separate us from the love of God.
> (Romans 8.39 REB)

'The kingdom
may appear quite insignificant,' he said,
'but watch how it grows!

'The kingdom
may appear to be hidden, even lost,
but all the time it is working
quietly, but effectively,
to transform the world.

'And the kingdom
is ever reaching out to enfold you,
and, like a net,
it catches fish of every kind;
so be warned, you may find yourself
in some very strange company.

'Recognize the kingdom
for what it really is
and you will allow nothing
to stand in the way of your possessing it.

'I tell you:
the wisest of teachers
will gladly return as a scholar to the kingdom,
that his teaching may be further enriched.'

**If there is one thing that is clear, Lord,
it is that we cannot pin down,
we cannot possess
or define limits for the kingdom.
But the kingdom can enfold us,
filling and enriching our lives.
Draw us, we pray, into that kingdom
and hold us there in your love for ever.**

The true nature of love

> He saw ... a woman bathing, and she was very beautiful. (2 Samuel 11.2 REB)
> May you, in company with all God's people, be strong to grasp what is the
> breadth and length and height and depth of Christ's love, and to know it,
> though it is beyond knowledge. (Ephesians 3.18-19 REB)

Don't call it love!

The passionate desire
which consumed David,
making him determined to possess Bathsheba,
come what may,
was so selfish, so blinded, so extreme,
that it led him to engineer the death
of the loyal, upright man who was her husband;
led him to calculated, cold-blooded murder.

Don't call it love!

The strength of love is gentleness,
the passion of love is not to grasp
but to give,
and the true lover
will not willingly do wrong to any.

Heavenly Father,
yours is an overwhelming love
which reaches out to the whole of creation
and embraces every human soul,
and through our Lord Jesus Christ
something of the heights and depths of that love
have become real to us.
May that love
not only enfold us,
but so possess us
and flow through us,
that we may share in the work
of making your love real for others
who as yet know little of what love really means.

You've only got to ask!

(12) July 24 - July 30. Year C

> Lord, show us your love and grant us your deliverance. (Psalm 85.7 REB)
> Be rooted in him, be built in him, grow strong in the faith as you were taught; let your hearts overflow with thankfulness. (Colossians 2.7 REB)
> Ask, and you will receive; seek, and you will find; knock, and the door will be opened to you. (Luke 11.9 REB)

So, I've only got to ask!
Well, if you put it that way, Lord,
I could really do with a new car,
the house needs decorating
and the kids keep on and on
about going to Disneyland
and having the latest in computers.

What's that you say?
I've got it wrong;
prayer is more than a shopping list
or a letter to Santa?
But what about the man in the parable —
I've read it, you know —
he knocked his friend up in the middle of the night,
and got all the loaves he wanted.

Oh,
you say he needed them to help somebody else;
does that make a difference then?

I suppose you couldn't arrange for a little something
to go through my wife's account?
No?
Hope you didn't mind my asking.

Lord, teach us to pray expectantly
for the things which belong to your kingdom,
for the things which will enrich the lives
of those we love — and those we ought to love.
Teach us how to pray expectantly
for the things that really endure,
the things which can enrich us all.

You must be joking!

> I will not let you go unless you bless me. (Genesis 32.26 REB)
> There is great grief and unceasing sorrow in my heart. I would even pray to be an outcast myself, cut off from Christ, if it would help my brothers, my kinsfolk. (Romans 9.2-3 REB)
> There is no need for them to go; give them something to eat yourselves. (Matthew 14.16 REB)

'You must be joking, Lord,
give them something to eat ourselves?
Just look at the size of the crowd,
you can't really expect us to do anything for them.
All we've got here
is five small loaves and a couple of fish,
that's the lot,
and even those aren't ours;
we're not miracle-workers you know.'

Those disciples must have wondered, doubted,
even as they obeyed Jesus
and told the people to prepare.
True, the Lord's blessing was with them,
but what would that count for
with so pitifully little to offer...?
Yet, as it turned out,
when they started distributing,
there was more than enough;
all were fed
and there was even something over.

Lord, we cannot expect to meet
all the needs that we learn about,
answer all the cries that come our way;
but give us the faith and the courage
to reach out and share what we have got,
be it much or little,
and when we have done all we can
let us be content to leave the end with you.

We need all the help we can get

(13) July 31 - August 6. Year B

> You are the man! (2 Samuel 12.7 REB)
> Spare no effort to make fast with bonds of peace the unity which the Spirit gives. (Ephesians 4.3 REB)

Prayer for help in daily living
Do not allow us, Lord,
while condemning the evil
in the world round about us,
to shut our eyes to the evil
in our own hearts.
However painful it may be,
make us face up to those things in our lives
which are wrong
and strengthen our will
not only to confess and seek forgiveness,
but, with your help,
to put wrong to right
however difficult that may be.

Prayer for help in seeking unity
O Holy Spirit of the One Eternal God
forgive us the pettiness and the small-mindedness
which lie behind so much that divides us;
above all forgive us the times
when we misuse your name
to justify our disunity,
claiming that we alone
have a proper understanding of your truth.
Take the scales from our eyes
that we may recognize that there is
'One body and one Spirit,
one Lord, one faith, one baptism;
one God and Father of all,
who is over all and through all and in all.'
And draw us closer to yourself
that we may experience more of the true unity
which is your gift to those who will receive it.

Far too late

> Were you not raised to life with Christ? Then aspire to the realm above.
> (Colossians 3.1 REB)
> 'Take life easy, eat, drink and enjoy yourself'. But God said to him, 'You fool,
> this very night you must surrender your life...' (Luke 12.19-20 REB)

Too late!
Of course it was too late,
it had been too late for years.
The young wife
who married him so joyously
had gradually become disillusioned
with his slavery to moneymaking,
his begrudging any item of expenditure
beyond the bare essentials,
and over the years
she had built a protective shell around herself.
His children
had taken the first opportunity to leave home
with scant love for the father
who had had so little time for them.
His neighbours
had long since
realized that they could look for
no neighbourly actions from him
and so left him to his own devices.
True, he had grown wealthy,
but he had done so
at the cost
of forgetting how to live.

**Lord, help us to enjoy the good things of life
without becoming enslaved by them.
Show us how the gifts you have for us
grow in the sharing
and help us to live lovingly and joyfully,
ever learning more of your way to abundant life.**

129

Walking on water

(14) August 7 - August 13. Year A

He came towards them, walking across the lake. (Matthew 14.25 REB)

Many of us are not quite sure what to make of nature miracles; questions surface, such as, did it really happen like this; is it maybe a misplaced resurrection appearance? We cannot know the answers, but we can thankfully grasp the inner truth of the story as Francis Thompson did when, out of the experience of being found by Christ when he was living rough on the Thames Embankment, he could write —

Yea, in the night, my Soul, my daughter,
Cry, clinging Heaven by the hems;
And lo, Christ walking on the water
Not of Gennesareth, but Thames!

Go not in search of miracles
so wasting precious years,
go not in search of miracles,
that search could end in tears.

Not in the supernatural
is Godhead to be found,
not in the supernatural,
but in the common round.

Too many search for miracles,
for troubles swept away,
but still the greatest miracle
is strength to live each day.

Miracles are everywhere,
wondrous gifts are free,
miracles are everywhere
for those with eyes to see.
(From *Cuthbert*)

May I never forget, Lord,
your promise to be with us, always;
may I never lose the confidence
that when my need is greatest
you will be there.

But, he's so ordinary!

> For in the Lord is love unfailing, and great is his power to deliver.
> (Psalm 130.7 REB)
> The bread which I shall give is my own flesh, given for the life of the world.
> (John 6.51 REB)
> Surely this is Jesus, Joseph's son! We know his father and mother.
> How can he say, 'I have come down from heaven'? (John 6.42 REB)
> Live in love as Christ loved you and gave himself up on your behalf.
> (Ephesians 5.2 REB)

'I am the bread of life.'
Bread!
Not cream cakes,
or a wildly exotic dish
conjured up to stimulate jaded palates,
but bread!

So the villagers of Nazareth said,
'But we know him.'
Their mistake was to believe
that God could only meet them
in the extraordinary;
not in something familiar,
like a neighbour,
like bread.

Christians gather for the Holy Meal
whether it be Eucharist, Mass,
Lord's Supper, Holy Communion,
the Breaking of Bread...
But even those
who share no such celebration,
may, in the everyday world,
beyond the walls of the church,
be nourished by the bread of life.

Lord, we thank you for the promise
that you will be with us
to nourish us and to renew our strength,
in each and every situation of life.
May we both recognize you and serve you
in whatever the everyday round may bring.

The law-abiding sinner

(14) August 7 - August 13. Year C

> Though your sins are scarlet, they may yet be white as snow. (Isaiah 1.18 REB)
> To him who follows my way I shall show the salvation of God.
> (Psalm 50.23 REB)
> Where your treasure is, there will your heart be also. (Luke 12.34 REB)

Sin figures on no charge sheet,
is not mentioned in a court of law.
Sin is a word we use
when we speak of our relationship with God,
or more particularly,
of those things we do,
or fail to do,
which hurt that relationship.

They may indeed be terrible things
which any right-minded person would condemn;
but we can also lead blameless lives
in the eyes of the law and of our friends
and still be sinners.

Sin is the barrier,
the mist,
the interference
which flows from us
and hinders or distorts communication
between us and the Almighty
and there is an awful lot of it about.

Lord, we betray you in following our own ways,
we deny you when we fail to follow yours,
and we mock you in our pride
and our self-centredness.
Lest we be utterly lost,
meet us with your forgiveness,
hold us in your strength
and renew us with your life.
Lord, you died that we might live;
live in us and through us,
for without you we cannot be saved
from the evil that would stifle us.

Surely not everybody

> For the gracious gifts of God and his calling are irrevocable ... God's purpose was to show mercy to all mankind. (Romans 11.29,32 REB)

I've got a problem, Lord.
Surely if even the best of us
were to enter heaven just as we are,
without you doing something to our lives,
we should soon turn heaven into hell.
But here you face us with the idea
that you don't only love the best of us,
you love us all!
Can we all be saved?
Are your love and your power so great
that you can take hold of us,
with all the evil we do
and make us new people?
All of us?
Is it possible that the whole of humanity
could be so changed
that we could live peaceably,
lovingly,
one with another,
that we could enter
your kingdom
without destroying it?
All of us?

Teach me, Lord, how to see
every man and every woman I meet
as someone dear to you,
someone you long to bring into your kingdom.
Strengthen my grasp on the truths
that have reached me through my Christian faith,
but let me also recognize
that, because we are so diverse,
you may have different ways
of reaching out to other of your children.
Save me from too hastily writing off
those different ways
as pagan, ungodly or false religion.

The skill to listen

> The fear of the Lord is the beginning of wisdom, and they who live by it grow in understanding. (Psalm 111.10 REB)
> Grant your servant, therefore, a heart with skill to listen. (1 Kings 3.9 REB)
> Use the present opportunity to the full, for these are evil days. (Ephesians 5.16 REB)

'Tell me what I shall give you,' said the Lord,
which opened up unlimited possibilities for Solomon.
What should a young king ask?
Victory in battle?
Long life?
Wealth?
Yet it was none of these
that Solomon sought;
instead, he asked the Lord
for 'A heart with skill to listen'.
Not something one would have expected
of a king having almost absolute power
over his subjects.

And what skill might we have asked,
given the opportunity?
Skill to plan,
skill to express ourselves,
skill to get things done?
But,
skill to listen?

Yet Solomon's request pleased the Lord.

That we may be ready to learn
from the wisdom of the past
and not least from the Scriptures;
that we may be ready in stillness and quietness
to wait for and listen to the inner voice;
that we may have all the time and the patience
we shall need to listen and pay heed
to what others would say to us;
Lord, grant us hearts with skill to listen.

Turn off the news

> He looked for justice but found bloodshed, for righteousness but heard cries of distress. (Isaiah 5.7 REB)
> Do you suppose I came to establish peace on the earth? No indeed, I have come to bring dissension. (Luke 12.51 REB)

Turn off the news!
Trouble, trouble, trouble.
Turn off the news!
Give something else a go.
Turn off the news!
Try another channel.
Turn off the news,
we don't want to know!

Turn off the news!
Best to keep your head down.
Turn off the news!
We'd rather have a soap.
Turn off the news!
The pictures are disturbing.
Turn off the news,
we need a little hope!

Famine, poverty, disease, everything is sour;
terrorism, civil war, gross abuse of power;
children, women, old and young,
dying by the hour.

Turn off the news!
We don't want others' problems.
Turn off the news!
Troubles only grow.
Turn off the news!
There must be something better.
Turn off the news,
we don't want to know!
(From *Upside Down And Inside Out*)

Lord God of Hosts, restore us, and make your face shine on us, that we may be saved. (Psalm 80.19 REB)

Part of the foundations

> I implore you by God's mercy to offer your very selves to him ... Let us use the different gifts allotted to each of us by God's grace. (Romans 12.1,6 REB)
> You are Peter, the Rock; and on this rock I will build my church. (Matthew 16.18 REB)

Peter!
The rock on which the Church is founded!
That puts him far beyond us,
and yet —
soon after he heard these words
Peter was told
he was speaking for the tempter,
and later,
under pressure,
he denied that he even knew Jesus.

So what was this rock?

Was Jesus saying
that the foundation of the Church
would be the underlying faith and love
of very ordinary men and women,
fallible, foolish, fearful, weak,
and, at times,
downright wrong?

Lord, we too would be built into your Church,
bringing to your service
such gifts as we have.
Others may have much more to offer,
but you tell us to come as we are,
to bring what we have got
and to use it to the glory of God.
So, Lord, take us
with all our limitations,
and by your grace transform us
into what you would have us be.

Dress for battle

Finally, find your strength in the Lord, in his mighty power. Put on the full armour provided by God, so that you may be able to stand firm against the stratagems of the devil. (Ephesians 6.10-11 REB)

We shall be fortunate indeed if there are not times when everything seems drab and grey, empty and meaningless, and we begin to wonder whether the struggle is worth it. This is when we need to look afresh to our armour. As Paul describes it, it is not the armour of an officer, but of a foot soldier, one who can seldom see where the battle is leading and who has to fight trusting in his commander, as we even more must trust in our Lord, in whom our ultimate victory is assured.

Be strong in the Lord,
use the armour God supplies.
Make integrity the cloak that you will wear.
Take truth as your belt,
put strong shoes on your feet;
to be a messenger of peace
must be your care.
Accept the gift
of the helmet of salvation
and the shield of faith
to guard you from the foe;
in your right hand take
the sword the Spirit gives you,
the Living Word
that none can overthrow;
and pray, pray, pray and ever pray
for yourself
and for God's people everywhere.
(From *Ragman*)

Moment of truth

(16) August 21 - August 27. Year C

I am not skilled in speaking; I am too young. (Jeremiah 1.6 REB)
There are six working days: come and be cured on one of them, and not on the sabbath. (Luke 13.14 REB)
You have come to Mount Zion, the city of the living God. (Hebrews 12.22 REB)

'I haven't the skill
or the experience,'
cried the young Jeremiah,
only one of the many excuses
which might be offered;
but when it comes,
the call to service is imperative
and there is no time for trivialities.

*You have come to Mount Zion, the city of the living God, the heavenly
Jerusalem, to myriads of angels, to the full concourse and assembly of
the firstborn who are enrolled in heaven...*

'There are six working days:
come and be cured on one of them,'
was the angry response of the president of the synagogue
when Jesus healed a woman
who had been crippled for eighteen years.
At all costs
follow the letter of the law;
refuse to consider the possibility
of fresh revelation.

*...and to God the judge of all, and to the spirits of good men made
perfect, and to Jesus the mediator of a new covenant.*

The psalmist, however, starts from trust.

*In you, Lord, I have found refuge;
let me never be put to shame.
By your saving power rescue and deliver me;
hear me and save me! (Psalm 71.1-2 REB)*

This prayer is answered before it is uttered.

The whole world?

> What will anyone gain by winning the whole world at the cost of his life?
> (Matthew 16.26 REB)

He knew how tempting that dream could be.
To win the world,
the whole world!
Hadn't he wrestled in the wilderness
with the idea of leading a great crusade,
overthrowing the might of Rome
and so establishing the kingdom?

The kingdom!
But whose kingdom?
There lay the rub,
> *'All these I will give you,*
> *if you will only fall down and do me homage.' (Matthew 4.9 REB)*

Hadn't that same temptation momentarily returned
when Peter sought to turn him
from the painful way which lay before him?

> *'Out of my sight, Satan;*
> *you are a stumbling block to me.*
> *You think as men think,*
> *not as God thinks.' (Matthew 16.23 REB)*

For Jesus knew that such power and glory
inevitably crumble;
that the Kingdom of God,
the only enduring kingdom
would be based
not on compulsion but on love,
not on grasping,
but on freely letting go.

> *If your enemy is hungry, feed him;*
> *if he is thirsty, give him a drink ...*
> *Do not let evil conquer you,*
> *but use good to conquer evil. (Romans 12.20-21 REB)*

Life is for living

(17) August 28 - September 3. Year B

> Every good and generous action and every perfect gift come from above ... look after orphans and widows in trouble. (James 1.17,27 REB)
> Nothing that goes into a person from outside can defile him; no, it is the things that come out of a person that defile him. (Mark 7.15 REB)

God of adventurous living,
you are always calling us to push back frontiers,
to re-evaluate rules and restrictions
and, above all else,
to reach out in loving concern
far beyond our own immediate circle.
You have given us life
and you call us
to take that life
and live it in such a way
that we may discover our full potential
as your people!

Lead us, we pray,
into generous, loving ways.
that we may really feel with others,
may willingly share their joys and sorrows
and seek to lighten oppressive loads
where we have means
and opportunity.

And so take hold of us
that there may be
less room in our living
for the things which defile us,
driven out
because we have become
more possessed of your spirit
and are living closer to your ways.

Two special occasions

> Do not neglect to show hospitality; by doing this, some have entertained angels unawares. (Hebrews 13.2 REB)
>
> Do not sit down in the place of honour. It may be that some person more distinguished than yourself has been invited. (Luke 14.8 REB)

A busy housewife
Why, what a pleasant surprise,
you've caught me in the middle of cooking,
but it's lovely to see you.
You won't mind joining me in the kitchen
and you'll stay for lunch?
No problem.
I've got a couple of friends coming,
they live alone,
one's just lost her husband.
No, there'll be plenty for all of us
and they'll love to meet you.

A disgruntled guest
They didn't have a seating plan
with neat little name cards,
so when the time came
I naturally took my place
at the top table.
It should have been a great occasion.
I had dressed with care as befitted my rank
and was just beginning to converse with our host
when his brother from up country,
whom he hadn't seen for years,
arrived unexpectedly.
I had no option but to give way to him.
By that time
the only seat left
was among the riff-raff,
with whom I have nothing in common.
It completely spoiled my meal
and gave ammunition
to some who do not wish me well.

Living in the plural

(18) September 4 - September 10. Year A

> Speak to the whole community of Israel... (Exodus 12.3 NJB)
> Love cannot wrong a neighbour; therefore love is the fulfilment of the law.
> (Romans 13.10 REB)
> Where two or three meet together in my name, I am there among them.
> (Matthew 18.20 REB)

This business of two or three
meeting together, Lord,
does that mean
that deciding what ought to be done
is not just a matter between you and me,
but involves other people as well?
Always?
Don't get me wrong,
I'm all for it in principle;
but you know only too well
there are occasions
when it isn't easy in church affairs
to get even two or three to agree together.
And what if there's a situation
where it's quite obvious
what ought to be done,
but I'm outvoted?

Lord?

Are you listening?

Teach us, we pray, the art
of listening to others
and also of listening with others
for your word.
And when our hearing is dimmed,
we receive confusing signals
and fail to agree;
teach us how to do so lovingly
and humbly,
that we may continue to seek together
until your will for us becomes clearer.

Who's right behind whom?

(18) September 4 - September 10. Year B

> So with faith; if it does not lead to action, it is by itself a lifeless thing.
> (James 2.17 REB)
> 'All that he does, he does well,' they said; 'he even makes the deaf hear and the dumb speak.' (Mark 7.37 REB)

It was Sunday:
so I went to church,
I prayed the prayers,
I sang the hymns,
I attended to the Scriptures,
I gave to the offertory
and I settled down to listen to the preacher.
It was warm and comfortable,
I was feeling good
and I said to the Lord,
— not out loud of course,
I wouldn't do a thing like that —
'You can count on me each Sunday, regular,
I'm right behind you.'

Then a funny thing happened.
I thought I heard the Lord answering me,
saying,
'Don't stay here too long will you?
I want you out in the world.
There's folks there needing a helping hand,
folks requiring encouragement,
folks who've had a raw deal,
folks needing a voice raised for them,
folks needing to know I love them.'
Puzzled, I said,
'Is that really you, Lord?
I can't see you anywhere.'
And the Lord answered,
'No, but that's because
I'm waiting for you outside,
you'll find when you get there
that *I'll* be right behind *you*.'

A recorded delivery

(18) September 4 - September 10. Year C

> Can I not deal with you as this potter deals with his clay? (Jeremiah 18.6 REB)
> If, then, you think of me as your partner in the faith, welcome him as you
> would welcome me. (Philemon v17 REB)

Philemon says farewell
Don't grieve, my son,
death holds no terrors for me;
why should I want to tarry
when so many
wait to greet me on the other side?

I gladly leave the estate
in your safe hands
knowing you will use well
those who work it for you.
Advice?
You'll have Onesimus;
though his primary concern
while she still lives
must be to manage
your mother's household;
that care I couldn't leave
in better hands.

One thing more.
The scroll which I have kept beside my couch,
the one Onesimus
so long ago
brought back with him from Paul...
give it into the safe keeping of the church;
I have hoarded it too long.
All that Paul wrote is precious
and should be shared.

Farewell, my son,
put love before all else,
and the grace of our Lord Jesus Christ
will always be with you.

This matter of forgiveness

> Who are you to pass judgment? ... For none of us lives, and equally none of us
> dies, for himself alone. If we live, we live for the Lord; and if we die, we die for
> the Lord. So whether we live or die, we belong to the Lord.
> (Romans 14.4,7-8 REB)
> Lord, how often am I to forgive my brother? (Matthew 18.21 REB)

Could I have a word
about this matter of forgiveness, Lord?
I do try to be understanding
and I'm truly ready
to forgive and forget;
well, quite a lot of the time I am;
but some people are absolutely impossible.
I mean, I'm only human,
surely there has to be a limit
to what's expected of me?
What's that you say,
you've never set any limit in my case?
But that's different,
isn't it?

Isn't it?

Compassionate, rescuing, forgiving God,
never let us take for granted
your loving, saving activity.
Never let us take for granted
the fact that despite all the evil we do
you still care for us,
still reach out to forgive and restore us.
So deal with us, we pray,
that we may have short memories
for any wrongs done to us
and long memories
for the sins you have forgiven.

Words, words, words

(19) September 11 - September 17. Year B

Wisdom cries aloud in the open air ... I would fill you with my spirit and make my precepts known to you. (Proverbs 1.20,23 REB)
What a vast amount of timber can be set ablaze by the tiniest spark! And the tongue is a fire. (James 3.5-6 REB)
But Jesus, turning and looking at his disciples, rebuked Peter. 'Out of my sight, Satan!' he said. 'You think as men think, not as God thinks.' (Mark 8.33 REB)

Impetuous as ever,
Peter blurted out
the first thing that came into his head.
Jesus was obviously making a big mistake,
and he must save him.
It was well meant;
nevertheless,
Peter got it disastrously wrong.

Yet what Peter said
was said in love;
unlike the inconsiderate,
angry, or downright malicious speech
of which James was writing.
James urged great care
in the use of language;
for whether for good or ill,
words once uttered
cannot be recalled.

**Words stream out
from radio and television,
from unsolicited mail,
from newspapers and magazines;
many more words than we can absorb,
many we would gladly do without.
Lord, do not let us get so overwhelmed by words
that we forget the importance of language.
Help us to choose our own words with care
so that we do not harm, or mislead.
May the words not only of our mouths,
but also of our pens and our computers
be always acceptable in your sight.**

God's answer to chaos

My people are foolish, they know nothing of me; senseless children, lacking all understanding, clever only in wrongdoing, but of doing right they know nothing. I looked at the earth and it was chaos. (Jeremiah 4.22-23 REB)
Here is a saying you may trust, one that merits full acceptance:
'Christ Jesus came into the world to save sinners'. (1 Timothy 1.15 REB)
'This fellow,' they said, 'welcomes sinners and eats with them.' (Luke 15.2 REB)

Loving God,
you make yourself known to us,
not in the trappings of imperial splendour,
but as a working shepherd
tirelessly seeking the lost.

You are the hope of all who have become lost
— following will o' the wisp pleasures,
— seeking after wealth or power,
— trapped in the web of their own cleverness,
— imprisoned in blind self-centredness.

You are the hope of all who have become lost
— overwhelmed by poverty or disease,
— hiding away because they fear rejection,
— rebelling against the injustices of life,
— consumed by bitterness or hatred.

You are the hope of each and every one of us,
— not deterred by the chaos we create,
— not deterred by the evil we do,
— not deterred by our wilfulness,
  our foolishness, our sheer stupidity.

Tireless, working, wounded shepherd,
ever loving, ever seeking,
you alone are our hope and our salvation.

Small-minded or big-hearted?

(20) September 18 - September 24. Year A

> That is the bread which the Lord has given you to eat. (Exodus 16.15 REB)
> Let your conduct be worthy of the gospel of Christ ... united in spirit and in mind, side by side in the struggle to advance the gospel faith. (Philippians 1.27 REB)
> Why be jealous because I am generous? (Matthew 20.15 REB)

Thankfulness

Heavenly Father, there are times when we feel
that we are getting rather a raw deal
compared with others we know
and we begin to feel very sorry for ourselves.
When those moments come,
take hold of us we pray;
turn us around,
and show us afresh the many, many things
for which we have cause to be thankful.
Teach us to genuinely rejoice
with those who have cause for rejoicing,
whilst at the same time valuing and giving thanks
for all the blessings that are already ours.

Openness

Holy Spirit, one with the Father and the Son,
forgive us when we try to take
little corners of your work
to make them our own.
Forgive us when we lose
our sense of proportion
and forget that we are called
to be part of a far greater purpose;
forget that we are called
to be partners in a great fellowship
of witnesses to the gospel faith.
Forgive us and so deal with us
that we may be more ready to welcome
the companions you give us to share in your enterprise,
and so guide us that our future conduct
may be more worthy
of the gospel of Christ our Lord.

Stand up to the devil

(20) September 18 - September 24. Year B

> With jealousy and rivalry come disorder and the practice of every kind of evil.
> Submit then to God. Stand up to the devil, and he will turn and run.
> Come close to God, and he will draw close to you. (James 3.16; 4.7-8 REB)
> They were silent, because on the way they had been discussing which of them
> was the greatest. (Mark 9.34 REB)

The devil?
Surely that's a very primitive idea;
like the tooth fairy,
completely out of place
in this modern world?

Yet there is a devil.
I know only too well
the devil within,
who prompts me
to put the worst construction
on words or actions I dislike,
who encourages impatience,
intolerance,
an exaggerated conception
of my own importance,
and,
oh, so very, very much more.

I would indeed stand up to this devil,
but I'd be hard put to it to do so,
if I were fighting him on my own.

**Lord, I know from bitter experience
how easily I can be led astray.
Help me, I pray,
to recognize the voice of the devil,
especially when he comes in the guise
of an angel of light.
Be with me in the battle
with the evil in my own soul
and keep reminding me
of the way you would have me go.**

149

Dishonesty praised

> The master applauded the dishonest steward for acting so astutely.
> (Luke 16.8 REB)

At first sight
it doesn't make sense
that he could tell the story of an absolute rogue
and praise him for his roguery.
And yet —
did Jesus have a twinkle in his eye,
maybe even an urge to laugh out loud
when he saw the consternation
on the faces of his disciples?

And did he go on to say,
'Look, this man faced a crisis.
True, it was one of his own making;
true, his solution was thoroughly dishonest,
but at least he acted
to resolve his dilemma;
he didn't just sit there
wringing his hands,
waiting for something to turn up.
Can't you see what you might achieve
working for God
if you showed the same determination
when you are about his business?'

**Initiating, enterprising God,
do not let us be seduced by the world,
but do show us how to take
the skills, the enterprise, the imagination,
the business acumen and the commitment
we see given to worldly enterprises,
to use in your Church,
in your way,
and for your purposes.**

Who does he think he is?

> Look to each other's interests and not merely to your own. (Philippians 2.4 REB)
> By what authority are you acting like this? (Matthew 21.23 REB)

A Pharisee
So, my friend, you find
this Jesus from Nazareth persuasive?
Oh, I freely admit
he has a way with him,
he has struck chords in my heart too.
There's much in what he says I'd welcome,
could I but believe it;
but no,
this man is dangerous,
cutting from beneath our feet
the very ground on which we stand.

Did you not hear him say,
here, in the Temple courts,
that tax collectors,
Roman lap dogs that they are,
and prostitutes —
prostitutes, I ask you! —
would enter the kingdom of God
before us;
before us, who shape our whole lives
by the law given by God through Moses?

Be reasonable,
can such a man, an artisan,
and from Nazareth of all places,
can such a man
be greater than Moses?
Can such a man
speak with the authority of God?

From failing to recognize you when you come
and from rejecting your truth
because it is unpalatable to us,
Good Lord, in your mercy, deliver us.

Properly and in order?

(21) September 25 - October 1. Year B

> Teacher, we saw someone driving out demons in your name, and as he was not one of us, we tried to stop him. (Mark 9.38 REB)

In a quiet corner of an English cathedral, final arrangements were being made with a group who had been invited to stage a dramatic production there. The wife of one of the cathedral clergy brought in tea, much to the disgust of the senior verger who was hovering near. 'She shouldn't do that,' he said in an angry whisper to one of the visitors. 'That's my business, not theirs. I don't interfere with them praying.'

We cherish our church, Lord,
it means a lot to us
and we wouldn't want it to come to any harm.
We have our own time-honoured ways
of ordering our affairs
and we take some pride in doing things
decently and in order.
We realize that there have to be changes,
that we must move with the times;
but we do try to handle such matters
as they arise, steadily,
and through the proper channels.

Now, our problem is this.
It has been pointed out to us
that you have been known
to call the most unsuitable,
sorry, we mean unlikely, people
to do things.
We can't pretend to understand how you choose folks,
but we wouldn't like to be found
standing in your way.
So what we are asking is this.
Would you please give us a little extra understanding
and the ability to recognize and welcome
anyone you might be calling
to your service in our area,
especially anyone
who isn't one of us?

The man who had everything

(21) September 25 - October 1. Year C

> The love of money is the root of all evil, and in pursuit of it some have wandered from the faith and spiked themselves on many a painful thorn.
> (1 Timothy 6.10 REB)
> There was once a rich man, who used to dress in purple and the finest linen, and feasted sumptuously every day. (Luke 16.19 REB)

He believed this life was all, with no hereafter,
so having wealth he used it to indulge himself.
If God disposed riches or poverty as he saw fit
then the rich man was more than content
with the Almighty's allocation.
When he died
the rich man was of course given
the funeral that befitted his status,
and an appropriately expensive memorial
and that should have been the end of the matter...

Surprised and unprepared,
the rich man woke to judgment
and found himself condemned.
He protested, of course;
if the Almighty had wanted him
to live differently
he should have let him know
in a more arresting way,
like sending someone back
from beyond the grave.

But answer came,
'If you would not live by the light you were given,
you would have paid no heed
even if someone had risen from the dead.'

There has been a rising from the dead,
but it does not convince sceptics
or silence opposition;
it is meaningful only to those
who seek to follow
where the risen Lord leads;
to them it is the ground of hope,
and the promise of salvation.

Back to basics

(22) October 2 - October 8. Year A

> God spoke all these words... (Exodus 20.1 REB)
> My one desire is to know Christ and the power of his resurrection.
> (Philippians 3.10 REB)
> This is the heir; come on, let us kill him, and get his inheritance.
> (Matthew 21.38 REB)

Look, Lord,
no offence meant,
but if you don't see much of us
in church these days
it's because
we've discovered freedom
in a big way.
It's great!
All the old restrictions
have gone,
it's a different world!
I mean, there are so many other things
we can do on a Sunday,
so many places to go,
so many new experiences to try out...

Are we happy?
That's a funny question, Lord.
I mean, what exactly is happiness?
But since you ask,
well, there is something we're still looking for;
not to worry though,
perhaps we'll find it next weekend.

What's that you say —
we've got a lot to learn
about the nature of freedom?
We need to get back to basics?
Us, Lord? Are you sure?

Lord, we would be truly free;
lead us, we pray, into the self-discipline,
the willing acceptance of your law,
and the commitment to your service
which make true freedom possible.

Lord of darkness and of light

> If we accept good from God, shall we not accept evil? Throughout all this, Job did not utter one sinful word. (Job 2.10 REB)
> ...he submitted to death; so that by God's grace his experience of death should benefit all humanity. (Hebrews 2.9 NJB)

You, our God,
are Lord of all that is,
and are to be found
in every imaginable experience.
Lord of darkness
and Lord of light.
Lord of the finite
and Lord of the infinite.
With us in failure
and with us in success.
With us in weakness
and with us in strength.
With us in sickness
and with us in health.

If ever we find ourselves
in such stifling gloom and desolation
that we feel
we have lost our hold on you;
break through our despair, we pray,
and remind us
that you have not
lost your hold on us.
Remind us
that you are not only in that gloom with us,
but that you know the way out
and will lead us through
until we reach the light once again.

Responsible service

(22) October 2 - October 8. Year C

> The Lord's love is surely not exhausted, nor has his compassion failed.
> (Lamentations 3.22 REB)
> Stir into flame the gift from God. (2 Timothy 1.6 REB)
> We have only done our duty. (Luke 17.10 REB)

That a flame may be kindled
God of power,
we pray that our lives
may be so touched by your Spirit
that dreams may be dreamt
and visions seen.
Help us to recognize
the work which you have for us,
and give us the will
to do with all our heart
whatever tasks may come to hand.

That we may be faithful servants
Father, in the brief time we are on this earth,
you call us to play our part
in the great succession of your people.
Help us to be faithful to that calling
so that we do not fail either
those who have gone before,
or those who shall follow after us
when our work is done.

That we may trust the inexhaustible God
However far we may have travelled
in our earthly journey, Lord,
let us not look wistfully backwards
but hopefully forwards,
in the confidence that whatever lies ahead
you will still be there in it with us.

All are worshippers

Come, make us gods to go before us. (Exodus 32.1 REB)
All that is true, all that is noble, all that is just and pure, all that is lovable and
attractive, whatever is excellent and admirable — fill your thoughts with
these things. (Philippians 4.8 REB)
The guests he had invited ... refused to come. (Matthew 22.3 REB)

The golden calf
appears in many guises,
each having its own devotees.

Nature abhors a vacuum,
and since deep within
each human heart
is planted a longing for God,
we seek objects for adoration
and offer worship,
if not to the Almighty,
then to idols of our own choosing.

Yet, though for a time
they may appear to satisfy our needs,
at the end,
all idols
leave their worshippers bereft.

Open-handed, generous God,
you invite us,
together with all and any
who will accept your invitation,
to share a feast.
Help us so to recognize
and seek after
whatever is lovable, attractive,
excellent and admirable,
that we may respond
to that invitation with joy
and share the delights of your table.

Marx had a point

> 'How hard it will be for the wealthy to enter the kingdom of God!' ... [They] said to one another, 'Then who can be saved?' (Mark 10.23,26 REB)

Karl Marx had a point
when he revolted against the bland assumption
that the gross inequalities of life,
especially the appalling working and living conditions
thrown up by the industrial revolution,
were inevitable.
That he also revolted against the image of God
projected by the rich and successful
when they went to worship
is not surprising.

William Booth saw the same conditions
and with passion he cried,
'While women weep as they do now, I'll fight;
while little children go hungry as they do now, I'll fight;
while men go to prison, in and out, in and out, I'll fight;
while there is a poor lost girl upon the street, I'll fight;
while there yet remains one dark soul without the light of God, I'll fight;
I'll fight to the very end.'
Impatient with the Church he knew,
and with a different vision of God,
Booth went out and founded the Salvation Army.

If our relationship to wealth is not right;
then neither our relationship to other human beings
nor our relationship to God, the Father of us all,
will be right either.

Lord, teach us to value
whatever wealth is ours,
be it little or much, as a trust,
that we may learn to handle it wisely,
generously and lovingly.
All that we have has come from you.
Show us how to use it to your glory.

Part of a community

Seek the welfare of any city to which I have exiled you, and pray to the
Lord for it. (Jeremiah 29.7 REB)
Show yourself worthy of God's approval, as a worker with no cause for shame.
(2 Timothy 2.15 REB)

Father of all people,
you reach out
to each and every one of us in love,
without making any distinctions.
Help us to learn from you
how to truly care for the well-being
of all our neighbours
and especially those we meet
in the course of our daily living.

We pray for all our elected representatives,
for civil servants and workers in local government,
for those engaged in health and emergency services,
for police and magistrates,
and for all engaged in the many
and varied forms of voluntary service.

We hold before you all involved
in our schools and colleges;
our shops, factories and offices;
those engaged in agriculture,
or who in other ways work the land
and care for the environment.

Show us all, we pray, how to play our part
in building a strong community
where there is much mutual support
and loving compassion;
a community which,
whether it recognizes it or not,
is permeated
and nourished by your Spirit.

Two kingdoms

(24) October 16 - October 22. Year A

> You turned from idols to be servants of the true and living God.
> (1 Thessalonians 1.9 REB)
> Then pay to Caesar what belongs to Caesar, and to God what belongs to God.
> (Matthew 22.21 REB)

Called to be citizens of heaven
we have not one loyalty, but two,
for we are also citizens of earth.
We have a part to play
in human affairs,
nor may we say
that the service of God
takes precedence;
for the God who meets us in Jesus Christ
is most likely to be found
in the rough and tumble of human life.

In the battle to create a just
and caring society,
in the struggle
to help the weak and the fragile,
we serve the God
who calls us
and will give us strength
to be witnesses
to the ways of the heavenly kingdom,
not so much in words
as in deeds of love.

**Lord, may we never forget
that the task of your Church
is not to withdraw from the world,
but to engage in the world;
that it is for us
to play our part as those
who joyfully acknowledge
that we are citizens
of both heaven and earth.**

Lord of all

> Then the Lord answered Job out of the tempest ... Where were you when I laid the earth's foundations? (Job 38.1,4 REB)

Lord of the storm clouds,
Lord of the sunlight;
Lord of the tides
in their ebbing and flowing;
Lord of the seasons
of seed time and harvest,
you are my Lord, my all.

Lord of the artisan,
Lord of the scholar;
Lord of the singing
and Lord of the silence;
Lord of the righteous
and Lord of the sinner,
suffer me not to fall.

Lord before all things,
Lord of the moment;
Lord of creation,
yet Lord of each heart-beat;
Lord the all-knowing
and Lord the all-loving,
you are my Lord, my all.

Hold me in sorrows,
hold me in laughter;
hold me in waking
and hold me in sleeping;
hold me in living
and hold me in dying;
suffer me not to fall.
(From *Cuthbert*)

161

A God who takes the initiative

(24) October 16 - October 22. Year C

> This is the covenant I shall establish ... I shall set my law within them, writing it on their hearts; I shall be their God, and they will be my people.
> (Jeremiah 31.33 REB)
> For the time will come when people will not stand sound teaching.
> (2 Timothy 4.3 REB)
> You hear what the unjust judge says. Then will not God give justice to his chosen? (Luke 18.6-7 REB)

Eternal God,
we sometimes delude ourselves
that we are coming to you,
seeking you,
discovering you;
when in truth
you are the one who takes the initiative,
reaching out to us in a love
which, however many times it is rejected,
has never wavered.

You have breathed the breath of life into us
and given us light to guide our way,
and when we ignore the light
and get lost in darkness,
you are the rescuer
who seeks us out
to set our feet on the path
once again.

More,
you have initiated a covenant relationship,
calling us into a partnership;
calling us to share
in an enterprise of love.

Help us so to recognize
the wonder of what you offer
that we may grasp it joyfully
and through good days and bad days alike
be held in that covenant relationship;
held secure in your love
against all adversity.

Links in a chain

> This is the land ... I have let you see it with your own eyes, but you will not cross over into it. (Deuteronomy 34.4 REB)
> Love the Lord your God with all your heart, with all your soul, and with all your mind ... Love your neighbour as yourself. (Matthew 22.37,39 REB)

**Lord, you have been our refuge
throughout all generations**

> You called Moses to the awesome task
> of leading disheartened slaves out of Egypt.
> Through him you made a covenant with them
> and built them into a people;
> but, in sight of the promised land,
> even Moses had to hand over his work to others.

**For in your sight a thousand years
are as the passing of one day
or as a watch in the night.**

> In Jesus Christ you came to us in a human life
> making a new covenant,
> dying for our sakes;
> yet still we wait to see the kingdom
> in all its fullness.

Lord, how long?

> What is that you say, Lord?
> That we should put our best
> into the living of each day as it comes,
> learn to love your ways
> and to love other men and women
> as you love them,
> and leave all else in your hands?

**May your saving acts appear to your servants,
and your glory to their children.**
(*Psalm 90.1,4,13,16* REB)

Living with the hiddenness of God

(25) October 23 - October 29. Year B

I know that you can do all things and that no purpose is beyond you.
(Job 42.2 REB)
Go; your faith has healed you. (Mark 10.52 REB)

I know that I cannot 'see' God,
nor can I begin to understand God's hidden purposes.
I have not eyes, ears or mind
able to comprehend
all the mysteries,
all the wonders of creation.

I cannot find the answers
to life's deepest questions.
I can only speak of the 'will of God'
in humility and awe.
The God who meets me in Jesus Christ
is not an open book to me,
but,
praise be,
I am an open book to God.

I do not need to pray
imploring God
to be active here,
or busy there in the world;
he is ever ahead of me;
but I do need to pray
that God will show me
where I should be active in his name.

It is not that I know God, but that God knows me;
not that I support God, but that God supports me.
This is the faith by which I live
and it is faith,
not knowledge,
that ultimately brings us home.

A life reviewed

> I have run the great race, I have finished the course, I have kept the faith.
> (2 Timothy 4.7 REB)
> God, have mercy on me, sinner that I am. (Luke 18.13 REB)

I have run the great race,' wrote Paul,
'I have finished the course.'
He didn't claim
that he had never stumbled on the way,
never strayed from the track,
never had to retrace his steps.
Nor did he claim
to have broken any records
or performed any special feats of endurance,
though he might well have done so.

No, the one claim he makes here
is that through thick and thin,
in good days and bad days alike,
he had stuck it out,
he had kept the faith.

Lord, there is much in my living
of which I am heartily ashamed;
truly I pray,
God, have mercy on me, sinner that I am;
but in that mercy
help me to pick myself up when I fall,
bring me back to the path when I stray
and so deal with me through all my failures
that, however much I stumble,
I may with your aid
finish my course,
I may keep the faith.

They had to get their feet wet

(26) October 30 - November 5. Year A

> Set foot in the waters of Jordan, then the waters of the Jordan will be cut off.
> (Joshua 3.13 REB)

At last they stood on the threshold of the promised land
but, to enter, they must first cross the Jordan
and the Jordan was fearsome in flood.
An earlier generation
had been saved from the pursuing Egyptians
by crossing the Red Sea on dry land.
Would God provide another miracle?

At the Lord's bidding they set out,
not waiting for the waters to subside,
but travelling in faith.
And that faith was tested
for, only when the priests carrying the Ark
stepped boldly into the flood,
getting their feet wet in the process,
did the waters dry up,
allowing the whole people to cross safely.

Give me, Lord,
the faith
and the courage
which don't wait for you
to smooth out the way ahead,
but are ready, at your bidding,
to take initiatives
which to other eyes
may appear foolish,
even hopeless;
when such venturing is what
the service of your kingdom requires.

Divisions can be overcome

> Your people will be my people, and your God my God. (Ruth 1.16 REB)
> You must love your neighbour as yourself. (Mark 12.31 REB)

There was little love lost
between Israel and Moab:
at best, suspicion and mistrust,
at worst, bitterness, hatred and war.
Thus it was no light decision for Ruth
to abandon her homeland and her people
to accompany Naomi
when she returned to Israel.

Only desperate need
had driven an Israelite family into Moab
but, having lived there,
even Naomi herself,
her menfolk dead,
could not be sure of the reception she would receive
as she came again to Bethlehem.

But the leap of faith was justified.
Naomi was welcomed
and Boaz the Israelite
took Ruth to be his wife.
Thus Ruth of Moab
became an ancestress
of David, Israel's greatest king,
and of God's Messiah.

Thank you, Lord,
for this, one of many signs
that racial differences
and community divisions
have no place
in your eternal kingdom.

We live by faith

(26) October 30 - November 5. Year C

There is still a vision for the appointed time ... Though it delays, wait for it.
(Habakkuk 2.3 REB)
Your instruction is ever just; give me understanding that I may live.
(Psalm 119.144 REB)
We pray for you always, that our God may count you worthy of your calling,
and that his power may bring to fulfilment every good purpose and every act
inspired by faith. (2 Thessalonians 1.11 REB)

We live by faith
in a loving, caring God,
however much the world we know
may appear to deny it.
And in that faith
the blind rejoice,
not because they see,
but because they shall see;
and the sick rejoice,
not because they have been healed,
but because the day will come
when they shall be whole again;
and the defeated rejoice
because God can pluck victory out of defeat;
and the bereaved rejoice,
not because sorrow has ended,
but because they look to the time
when death will have no more dominion.

Lord, we pray for the coming of the day
when those who hunger to see right prevail
shall be fed,
those who thirst for the things of God
shall be satisfied,
those who mourn the world's sorrows
shall be comforted,
and those who await the coming of the kingdom
shall find the kingdom already present in their hearts.

Choose!

> Choose here and now whom you will serve. (Joshua 24.15 REB)
> They were charged to put their trust in God, to hold his great acts ever in mind
> and to keep his commandments. (Psalm 78.7 REB)
> Five of them were foolish, and five prudent. (Matthew 25.2 REB)

Of course it is difficult
trying to answer the call
to be 'the people of God';
but difficulty and opportunity
are often two sides of the same coin
and this is an exciting time to be alive.
Gone are the false certainties.
Gone is the belief
that the world is automatically getting better and better.
We are living through great upheaval and change
and what God will bring to birth in the coming years
may well be something of which few could even dream.

If we would serve the Almighty
it must be as Abraham did,
ever following a half-heard voice,
ever building new altars to a half-known God;
always travellers,
always pilgrims,
always seeking the land of promise.

I cannot prove that God exists.
I cannot prove that love is stronger than hate.
I cannot prove that the kingdom of God is invincible.
I can only affirm that I believe in a God
who has given us power to choose
and calls us to stake our lives
on the universe being his universe
and the way of Christ —
the way of the leader
who washes his disciples' feet
and gives his life that others may live —
being the way of life.

Reckless extravagance

(27) November 6 - November 12. Year B

> Unless the Lord builds the house, its builders labour in vain.
> (Psalm 127.1 REB)
> Presently there came a poor widow who dropped in two tiny coins, together
> worth a penny. (Mark 12.42 REB)

Quietly, almost ashamedly,
she dropped into the treasury
the only coins she possessed.
Then she slipped away
and for her that was the end of the matter.
She would probably have been horrified
to think she had been noticed,
even more horrified
if she had realized that she would be quoted
around the world
and across the ages.

Quoted, or misquoted:
for the point that Jesus was making
was not that every little helps —
God is grateful for anything we may bring along,
however small —
but that here was a woman
who might well wonder
where her next meal was coming from
and yet who,
in reckless extravagance,
gave everything she had got.

Lord, I try to handle the money I have
responsibly, with careful budgeting,
but if a situation suddenly calls
for a burst of unplanned giving,
don't let me stifle generosity with prudence,
for you held nothing back
when you gave yourself for me.

When our world is in ruins

> The splendour of this latter house will surpass the splendour of the former, says the Lord of Hosts. (Haggai 2.9 REB)
> I beg you, my friends, do not suddenly lose your heads.
> (2 Thessalonians 2.1-2 REB)
> God is not God of the dead but of the living; in his sight all are alive.
> (Luke 20.38 REB)

Many despaired
as they stood amid the ruins of the Temple,
but the word that came through Haggai
was one of encouragement,
coupled with the challenge
to cease looking back
and to start the work of rebuilding.

Different uncertainties
faced the Thessalonian congregation.
Was the end of the age upon them?
If so, how should they prepare to meet it?
For them the need was to stop speculating,
to live solidly in the present
and to do each day
the work that came to hand.

To those who saw death as final,
Jesus affirmed that before God all are alive,
putting our lives in a very different perspective.

Father, we thank you
for those who, standing among the ruins
of all they have held dear,
are able to prepare to start building afresh;
for those who, facing great uncertainties
are able to give all they have
to the living of the day in hand;
for those who, confronted with death,
are sustained by the faith
that death is not an end but a beginning.
Father, give us the faith
and the will to be numbered among them.

The 'Day of the Lord'

> The day of the Lord comes like a thief in the night. (1 Thessalonians 5.2 REB)
> Their master returned, and proceeded to settle accounts with them.
> (Matthew 25.19 REB)

When the 'day of the Lord' comes,
sudden
and unexpected —
will it be a moment of revelation
when I am confronted
with the unimagined implications
of things I have done
or left undone?
Will I see as never before
opportunities that were wasted
and gifts that were inadequately employed?

The prospect of the 'day of the Lord'
would be grim indeed
were it not that the Lord
is Jesus who,
though he comes in judgment
comes also
as
the Saviour of the world.

God did not choose us to suffer his anger,
but to possess salvation through our Lord Jesus Christ,
who died for us in order that we might live together with him.
(1 Thessalonians 5.9-10 GNB)

Lord, let me not live in an unholy fear of judgment,
neither let me live complacently
because you come as Saviour;
but help me so to respond
to the warmth of your love
that I may make the most of the life
I have been given
and have something to offer back to you
when the 'day of the Lord' comes.

Holding on

> Hannah rose in deep distress, and weeping bitterly stood before the Lord and prayed to him ... Eli took her for a drunken woman. (1 Samuel 1.9,13 REB)
> We should not stay away from our meetings, as some do, but rather encourage one another, all the more because we see the day of the Lord drawing near. (Hebrews 10.25 REB)
> Not one stone will be left upon another ... these are the first birth-pangs of the new age. (Mark 13.2,8 REB)

So there are times when the Church
looks tired, old-fashioned,
totally depressing
and on the way out?
But this is nothing new!

Shiloh was a run-down sanctuary
when Samuel was born —
In those days the word of the Lord was rarely heard,
and there was no outpouring of vision. (1 Samuel 3.1 REB)
Yet it was in Shiloh
that the child Samuel heard God's call and responded.

The writer of the *Letter to the Hebrews*
was concerned about poor church attendance
and that was the first century!
Yet the church grew,
continued through the ages
with saints and martyrs,
and today the call comes
to us to hold fast
and play our part in the succession of witnesses.

Lord, help us to put aside all distractions
that we may indeed worship you
with heart, soul, mind and strength.
Whatever else changes,
you are utterly dependable;
even when we forget you,
you do not forget us.
Glory be to you, our God and Father
for in you alone is our hope,
in you alone can we trust.

Keeping on course

(28) November 13 - November 19. Year C

> See, I am creating new heavens and a new earth! (Isaiah 65.17 REB)
> Anyone who will not work shall not eat. (2 Thessalonians 3.10 REB)
> Take care that you are not misled ... By standing firm you will win yourselves
> life. (Luke 21.8,19 REB)

The messengers of the Risen Christ
went out, and through the preaching of the gospel
lives were transformed.
In many of the new Christian fellowships
loving concern for their poorest members
led to a pooling of resources
and the free provision of food and other necessities
according to need.
Understandably, this drew
some attracted by the easy pickings
and others who wrongly assumed
that if a new age was coming
all they had to do was sit back and wait for it.

The truth is more complex.
We are called to live
as citizens of the new age
in the midst of the old
and there is nothing easy about that.
Worthwhile, yes,
rewarding, yes,
but never easy
and sometimes extremely painful.

**Lord, you have called us
to live as citizens of your kingdom,
however hard that may be at times.
To help us,
you have promised your presence
and you always keep faith.
Give us the strength, we pray,
to keep faith with you
this day and all our days.**

A sheep or a goat?

> Now I myself shall take thought for my sheep and search for them.
> (Ezekiel 34.11 REB)
> His mighty strength was seen at work when he raised Christ from the
> dead. (Ephesians 1.19-20 REB)
> He will place the sheep on his right hand and the goats on his left.
> (Matthew 25.33 REB)

Am I a sheep or a goat?
One thing is clear from this story,
it doesn't do to start counting 'Brownie Points'
— how many times I've been to church
— or how many old ladies I've helped across the road.
The folks who did this —
and for that reason
were confident that they were sheep —
were in for a big surprise.

My hope lies
not in any virtue I might have
but in the nature of the shepherd
who seeks even the most foolish of his sheep
at cost
and in love.

I shall search for the lost,
recover the straggler,
bandage the injured,
strengthen the sick,
leave the healthy and strong to play,
and give my flock their proper food. (Ezekiel 34.16 REB)

Lord God,
source of our being,
ground of our hope;
you know us
so much better than we know ourselves,
you know all our weaknesses,
all our follies;
deal graciously with us, we pray,
and despite our many shortcomings
bring us within your fold
and make us whole.

Behind all and in all

(29) November 20 - November 26. Year B

'I am the Alpha and the Omega,' says the Lord God, who is, who was, and who is to come, the sovereign Lord of all. (Revelation 1.8 REB)
My task is to bear witness to the truth. (John 18.37 REB)

How did it all begin,
the world,
the universe?
Did anything exist before creation?
And what is 'matter'?
If everything we know
originated in a 'big bang',
what were the ingredients
of such a mighty explosion?
What triggered it?
Whose finger was on the button?

In Genesis we read that before all else
the Spirit of God moved over the raw material
from which all creation would spring.
We read,
'In the beginning, God...'
I have yet to hear
a better explanation.

Lord, by whose Spirit
all that was,
all that is,
and all that shall be
has its being;
teach us to look for you
in all created things
and to handle all created things as holy.
Lead us through the wonders of creation
back to you
in whom alone
all things find meaning and purpose.

And all shall be well

> I myself shall gather the remnant of my sheep. (Jeremiah 23.3 REB)
> Making peace through the shedding of his blood on the cross.
> (Colossians 1.20 REB)
> Jesus said, 'Father, forgive them; they do not know what they are doing.'
> (Luke 23.34 REB)

If you cried out in rage
I too could storm,
if you condemned me, Lord,
I could resist,
if you ignored my fault
I could stay blind,
but you forgive.

If you made lightning fall
I too could burn,
if you destroyed your foes
I too could hate,
if you abandoned me
I could go hide,
but you forgive
— you forgive!
(From *One Friday*)

Lord Jesus Christ,
we come with all our hurts,
all our disappointments,
all our awareness of failure,
all our sense of injury,
all our pent-up bitterness,
dislikes and hatreds
and yes,
all our sin.
Lord, we pray that we may experience
the cleansing and the healing
of your wonderful, costly forgiveness,
that we may be freed from these burdens
and go out to live as whole people
for your sake and in your name.

Saints alive

All Saints. Years A, B & C

> I looked and saw a vast throng, which no one could count, from all races and tribes, nations and languages. (Revelation 7.9 REB) Year A
> Blessed are those whose hearts are pure; they shall see God. (Matthew 5.8 REB) Year A
> The souls of the just are in God's hand; no torment will touch them ... they are at peace. (Wisdom 3.1,3 REB) Year B
> The Spirit is the guarantee that we shall receive what God has promised his people. (Ephesians 1.14 GNB) Year C

Part of a great family   am 2000-am

Heavenly Father, we thank you
that in the immensity of your love
we are part of a great family
drawn from every age
and from every part of the earth.
We thank you
that, many as we are,
you assure us
through our Lord Jesus Christ
that to you
each and every one of us is precious.
Let the awareness
of being part of a great company,
and the assurance that your love
is always about us
give us a renewed sense of purpose
in our daily living.
May we willingly undertake
whatever you put into our hands
and serve you joyfully in all things
whether they be great or small.

Make us worthy
Lord, when we remember
those who, age by age,
have witnessed to the faith,
often facing hardship, misrepresentation,
imprisonment, torture, death;
we become aware of the shoddiness
of much of our own living.
Lord, have mercy upon us,
Christ, have mercy upon us,
Lord, have mercy upon us.

Honouring our heritage
With deep thanksgiving
we honour those who have served you
in former days,
a great company of saints.
Yet, though we cherish the past,
remind us again
that we must not seek to reproduce the past;
that each generation
is presented with new challenges,
new tasks.
Save us from the error
of appealing to the past
to justify resistance to change
and remind us afresh
that some of the greatest moments in past days
were those when you raised up men and women
ready to break new ground,
ready to reach out into the unknown
in answer to your call.

Index of Biblical References

Old Testament

Index of Biblical References

Index of Biblical References

Index of Biblical References

Index of Biblical References

Index of People and Places

Index of People and Places